ARBITRATION:
Essential Concepts

Steven C. Bennett, Esq.

2002

ALM Publishing

New York, New York

Cover Design: *Michael Ng*

Interior Page Design & Production: *Amparo Graf*

Library of Congress Control Number: 2002102511

Bennett, Steven C., 1957-

Dedication

To:
Suzanne, Danielle and Nicole,
with love and appreciation.

Dedication

Acknowledgment

I wish to acknowledge, gratefully, the support and encouragement provided by my law firm for teaching and writing endeavors. The views expressed in this book, however, are solely my own, and should not be attributed to the law firm or its clients.

I especially wish to acknowledge Fredrick E. Sherman, my mentor, partner and co-teacher, for his vast insight into the subject matter of this book.

Request for Comments

It is the author's fervent hope that this book will be of use to lawyers, law students and business people interested in learning the fundamentals of arbitration law. Comments about the book, including suggestions for additions to any future editions, are welcomed. Comments may be addressed to *scbennett@jonesday.com*.

CONTENTS

Chapter 1

INTRODUCTION TO AND A BRIEF HISTORY OF ARBITRATION

In today's economy, most lawyers, and many business people, sooner or later will encounter arbitration. The concept may arise in the context of negotiating a deal. One or the other party may suggest that, in lieu of litigation, arbitration be chosen as the method for resolving disputes under the agreement. Even if there is no agreement to arbitration in advance, parties may decide after a dispute arises to submit the dispute to arbitration. Certain standard forms of agreement, moreover, may contain arbitration clauses. Thus, for better or worse, the parties litigating the dispute will (unless otherwise agreed) be required to proceed through arbitration. Many courts, moreover, are experimenting with court-sponsored arbitration as a method of decreasing their burgeoning case-loads.

Despite the widespread use and involvement in arbitration, for most lawyers and business people, arbitration is not a daily event. As a result, although they may have vague familiarity with the process, they do not necessarily have mastery of the essential concepts and materials of arbitration.

This book is meant as an introduction to the essential concepts and materials of arbitration. Lawyers and business people, armed with a more comprehensive understanding of the arbitration process and law, should be able to approach their next arbitration-related issue with increased confidence and insight. This book is meant, moreover, as a shelf reference, designed to provide a brief refresher on these essential concepts and materials whenever the need arises. Finally, law students who seek a primer on arbitration, as an adjunct to the case-books used in courses on the law of arbitration, may find this book useful.

Arbitration as a Form of ADR

Arbitration is a form of Alternative Dispute Resolution (ADR), a concept that includes an array of procedures for private resolution of disputes. ADR is a loose term, encompassing various forms and procedures, sponsored by various organizations, with various rules. The one thing common to these many ADR forms is that they all are generally private dispute resolution methods, which parties may choose as an alternative to conventional litigation, and fashion to fit their particular needs.

One classic form of ADR includes settlement discussions between parties or their counsel, which may occur before or during litigation proceedings. Such discussions often lead to non-judicial resolution of disputes.

Another classic form of ADR is mediation, in which a neutral attempts to facilitate settlement of a dispute by listening to the parties (together and/or separately) and uncovering the strengths and weaknesses of their positions, so that they can more rationally discuss settlement. A mediator may gather additional information (reviewing documents, receiving briefing positions from the parties, or even interviewing witnesses), and may suggest solutions to the dispute. The mediator's suggestions are generally not binding on the parties.

A final often-used form of ADR is arbitration. An arbitrator or panel of arbitrators conducts an information-gathering process, which may include document exchange, briefing and testimony of witnesses. The arbitrator's decision is generally binding on the parties, subject to limited review by a court on motion to confirm or vacate the arbitration award.

These classic forms may be modified to create new forms. For example, in "mediation/arbitration," a mediator is authorized to attempt to fashion a settlement of the case. If no settlement is reached, the mediator serves as the arbitrator for the matter. In a "mini-trial," a mediator or advisory "jury" hears a summary version of each party's case, and renders a non-binding advisory decision, which may help the parties to reach consensus on a settlement.

This book focuses on arbitration, in its classic form. Practitioners may encounter many variations on the classic arbitration form (including valuation experts, construction dispute resolution boards, and a host of other forms). The concepts, and the law, summarized in this book generally apply to all these forms of arbitration.

Sponsoring Organizations

Sponsoring organizations vary in their approaches, even when they implement classic forms of arbitration. The rules of the International Chamber of Commerce (Paris) and London Court of International Arbitration (London), for example, favor a European approach to issues like discovery. By contrast, the American Arbitration Association (New York) follows an American approach. There are dozens of additional sponsoring organizations in the United States and throughout the world. Many sponsoring organizations offer specialized rules adapted to a specific kind of dispute (e.g., National Association of Securities Dealers, World Intellectual Property Organization), as well as lists of potential arbitrators with experience in particular subject matters, and specialized geographic or language backgrounds.

only
only is
Issue

Parties frequently agree to *ad hoc* arbitration without the supervision of any sponsoring organization. In other instances, parties may agree to arbitration under the auspices of a sponsoring organization but with their own individually designed processes. Even if a sponsoring organization is used, parties are generally free to agree to specialized rules and to choose arbitrators with experiences and skills that meet their needs.

Why Arbitrate?

Parties may choose to arbitrate for any number of reasons. Some of the most popular reasons include:

PRIVACY

Arbitration proceedings are generally private. Pleadings are not publicly filed, arbitration sessions are closed, and decisions are not released to anyone other than the parties. When, however, arbitration breeds litigation (either at the beginning of the process, when one party challenges the authority to arbitrate, or at the conclusion of the process, when a party challenges the award), the privacy of the arbitration may be invaded, because the litigation proceedings will generally be open.

CHOICE OF DECISION-MAKER

Generally, the parties to an arbitration have significant say in choosing the persons who will serve as arbitrators. The parties may simply agree on an arbitrator. If they cannot, they may make use of a sponsoring organization, which will typically provide them with lists of potential arbitrators from which they can choose. The ability to choose an arbitrator is especially important for certain kinds of complex or technical matters, where most judges and juries will have no expertise in the area.

FLEXIBLE RULES

The rules in litigation are designed for all cases. In arbitration, the parties may choose the rules and procedures that they believe will best achieve a fair and efficient resolution of their dispute. The arbitrator also generally enjoys great discretion to fashion a process that best meets the needs of the parties, and the case.

REDUCED COSTS AND TIME TO DECISION

Although there is little hard evidence to prove that arbitration is necessarily faster or cheaper, on average, than litigation, many parties prefer arbitration for these reasons. Arbitration typically employs streamlined procedures (relatively little discovery, for example), which can improve the efficiency of the decision-making process.

RECOVERY OF COSTS

The American rule on fee-shifting typically provides that each party bears its own costs and attorneys' fees in litigation. Arbitration proceedings often reverse that rule, adopting a "loser pays" system. Many parties believe that such a system discourages frivolous claims, and encourages settlement.

BUSINESS-LIKE ATMOSPHERE

Although many arbitrators are lawyers (and some are ex-judges), they need not be. Many parties choose arbitrators for their technical expertise, rather than legal knowledge (or choose to form an arbitration tribunal with a mixed group of arbitrators, some of whom may have no legal background). Arbitration proceedings typically take place in private conference rooms, around a table, rather than in a court-like setting. Rules of evidence and procedure are relaxed. As a result, the process may seem more business-like, and less lawyerly, than ordinary litigation.

FINALITY AND ENFORCEMENT

Rights of appeal from an arbitration decision are very limited. Mere factual error, and even error of law, typically do not suffice to upset an award. As a result of the Federal Arbitration Act, and equivalent state statutes and international treaties, moreover, arbitration awards are often as easy to enforce (and, in some instances, easier to enforce) as decisions from judges and juries.

NEUTRAL FORUM

Left to themselves, most parties to a lawsuit would prefer to litigate in their "home" court, in their city and state, before judges and juries they understand, and using rules with which they are familiar. Because both sides have the same home court instinct, often the only neutral forum on which they can agree is arbitration. The choice of arbitration avoids the possibility of a "race to the courthouse" and the possibility of dueling litigations in separate jurisdictions.

Not a Panacea

Despite its many advantages, arbitration is not necessarily the best form of dispute resolution in every case. Parties choose not to arbitrate for any number of reasons, including:

♦ Limitations on discovery
♦ Difficulty in acquiring preliminary relief
♦ Relaxed standards for decision, and limited review

Many parties do not arbitrate simply because the arbitration alternative has never been presented to them. Indeed, despite nearly a century of experience with modern arbitration forms, arbitration remains as only a relatively modest part of the decision-making system in the United States. Millions of cases are filed in state and federal courts each year, while arbitration proceedings generally number in the tens of thousands. Although arbitration is not a panacea, the history of arbitration is still being written. Judges, legislators, practitioners and academics are increasingly paying attention to the potential value of arbitration.

A Brief History

Arbitration, the submission of disputes to resolution before a private tribunal or decision-maker, has ancient origins. Arbitration is mentioned in Greek mythology and in the Bible.

Arbitration was an established method of dispute resolution among merchants and in the maritime industry in pre-colonial England. The American colonists brought the system with them when they landed in the New World. In the American colonies before the revolution, arbitration played an important role in resolving disputes. Arbitration was prized as an inexpensive, expeditious and private method of dispute resolution. Enforcement of arbitration decisions, however, was voluntary, and arbitration depended on community ties and pressures for its effectiveness.

As the industrial revolution developed, and the population grew and migrated, weakened community ties made voluntary, unenforceable arbitration less attractive. In some industries, informal oral submission to arbitration gave way to formal written submission, backed by conditioned bonds or promissory notes, which could be drawn upon to satisfy an arbitration award. In 1768, the New York Chamber of Commerce established the first permanent board of arbitration in the United States. By 1817, the securities industry adopted a constitution that included the first comprehensive arbitration clause. Such forms, however, were not available to all levels of disputants. The unavailability of enforceable equitable relief in arbitration also made arbitration less attractive as a dispute resolution tool.

The native difficulty in administering private dispute resolution was mirrored by judicial antipathy toward the process. Justice Story, in a famous case, suggested that arbitrators have "no authority whatsoever" to administer oaths or to compel the attendance of witnesses, and are "not ordinarily well enough acquainted with the principles of law or equity" to administer justice effectively. See *Tobey v. County of Bristol*, 23 F. Cas. 1313, 1321 (C.C.D. Mass. 1845). Thus, under the common law rule, a party to an arbitration agreement could revoke the agreement at any time, up to the point that the arbitrator rendered a decision. The unenforceability of arbitration contracts led to forum-shopping, and could render arbitration clauses meaningless.

The dawn of the twentieth century brought new economic and political developments, which made arbitration an increasingly attractive dispute-resolution alternative. One was the rise of the organized labor movement. Both unions and management increasingly recognized that all parties needed a speedy, inexpensive and fair method to resolve the numerous disputes that arose in the context of modern industrial operations. At the same time, the expansion of social welfare regulation and administrative power required the development of quasi-judicial administrative law proceedings, which very much resembled arbitration.

Fast on the heels of these pro-arbitration developments, in 1920, the New York legislature adopted the first American statute recognizing the validity, and enforceability, of arbitration agreements. In 1925, the United States Congress enacted the Federal Arbitration Act (FAA), which was modeled on the New York arbitration statute. The fundamental premise of the New York statute, and the FAA, was that agreements to submit disputes to arbitration should be as enforceable as any other contracts. The FAA has analogues in most states based on the Uniform Arbitration Act, formulated in 1955.

Despite the language and purpose of these statutes, for many years courts remained skeptical toward arbitration. In *Wilko v. Swan,* 346 U.S. 427, 74 S.Ct. 182, 98 L.Ed. 168 (1953), for example, the Supreme Court declined to compel arbitration of claims under the Securities Act of 1933, brought by an investor who had signed agreements requiring arbitration of any disagreements with his brokerage firm. The Court questioned the competence of arbitrators to resolve Securities Act claims effectively and concluded that "the protective provisions of the Securities Act require the exercise of judicial direction to fairly assume their effectiveness."

Cracks in the Supreme Court's antipathy toward arbitration agreements first began to appear in the area of international arbitration. Recognizing that arbitration can be an especially desirable method of resolving international disputes (where otherwise local judicial prejudice and race-to-the-courthouse litigation might hamper an effective dispute resolution), the Court compelled international arbitration, even where it involved claims under the Securities Exchange Act of 1934 or the federal antitrust laws. See *Scherk v. Alberto-Culver Co.,* 417 U.S. 506, 94 S.Ct. 2449, 41 L.Ed.2d 270 (1974), and *Mitsubishi Motors Corp. v. Soler Chrysler-Plymouth, Inc.,* 473 U.S. 614, 105 S.Ct. 3346, 87 L.Ed.2d 444 (1985).

Once the cracks appeared, the Court's decisions increasingly supported arbitration, even outside the international context. In 1989, the Court overruled its *Wilko* decision. See *Rodríguez de Quijas v. Shearson/American Express,* 490 U.S. 477, 109 S.Ct. 1917, 104 L.Ed.2d 526 (1989). Subsequent decisions have consistently confirmed that the FAA establishes a liberal federal policy favoring the enforcement of arbitration agreements. The Court has recognized that the FAA applies in state as well as federal courts, and withdraws the power of the states to require a judicial forum for the resolution of claims that parties have agreed to resolve by arbitration.

The pendulum has swung so far in the direction favoring arbitration that, increasingly, courts are directing the use of non-binding arbitration and other forms of ADR as an adjunct to court processes. Courts have always had inherent power to form creative procedures for dispute resolution, which can include ADR. In 1983, however, Rule 16 of the Federal Rules of Civil Procedure was amended to grant express authority to federal district courts, at pre-trial conferences, to consider "settlement and the use of special procedures to assist in resolving the dispute when authorized by statute or local rule." In 1990, Congress required federal district courts to implement "civil justice expense and delay reduction" plans. The congressional statement of findings for the Expense and Delay Reduction statute noted that "effective litigation management and cost and delay reduction principles" may incorporate a variety of interrelated programs, including "utilization of alternative dispute resolution programs in appropriate cases."

In 1998, Congress enacted the Alternative Dispute Resolution Act, which required every federal district court to authorize, by local rule, "the use of alternative dispute resolution processes in all civil actions," and to designate a judge or other employee to be knowledgeable in ADR practices. Congress required each federal district court to offer at least one form of ADR, including such procedures as mediation, early neutral evaluation, minitrial, or arbitration, but permitted each court to exempt specific cases, or categories of cases, as not "appropriate" for ADR. Congress required that neutrals used in ADR processes be adequately trained, and specifically suggested training of magistrate judges, or use of professional neutrals from the private sector. Congress permitted referral to arbitration, where parties consented, but only in cases valued at less than $150,000 in damages.

Individual federal district courts have adopted many forms of ADR. State courts have also been experimenting with various forms of ADR. Many other federal and state statutes, such as the Y2K Act of 1999, moreover, have been designed to encourage ADR in various areas.

Today, most lawyers, and certainly most litigators, sooner or later will encounter ADR processes, and arbitration in particular, in one form or another. Knowledge of the basic principles and practices of arbitration law has become essential.

Chapter 2

DOMESTIC ARBITRATION STATUTES

The Federal Arbitration Act

It is not an overstatement to say that the Federal Arbitration Act (FAA) is the single most important element of modern American arbitration law and policy. The FAA was enacted in 1925 in response to judicial antipathy to the concept of arbitration. The FAA places agreements to arbitrate on the same footing as any other contracts, and provides specific mechanisms for enforcing arbitration agreements, and the awards that are issued by arbitrators. The FAA has spawned parallel state legislation. A portion of the FAA, adopted in 1970, implements an international convention on the recognition and enforcement of arbitral awards. That portion of the FAA is addressed in the chapter dealing with international arbitration.

Scope of the FAA

The FAA applies to any "written provision in any maritime transaction or a contract evidencing a transaction involving commerce" in which the parties have agreed to "settle by arbitration a controversy thereafter arising out of such contract or transaction," or an "agreement in writing to submit to arbitration an existing controversy arising out of such a contract [or] transaction."

"Maritime transactions" include charter parties, bills of lading for water carriers, and the like. "Commerce" means "commerce among the several states or with foreign nations." Thus, the FAA is based on the broad congressional power to regulate admiralty jurisdiction and interstate commerce.

The FAA, however, contains a limitation on this broad coverage. The Act states that "nothing herein contained shall apply to contracts of employment of seamen, railroad employees, or any other class of workers engaged in foreign or interstate commerce." Although this limitation has generally been confined to transportation workers, at least some courts suggested that the FAA did not apply to contracts of employment. In *Circuit City Stores, Inc. v. Adams,* 532 U.S. 105, 121 S.Ct. 1302, 149 L.Ed.2d 234 (2001), however, the Supreme Court ruled that the FAA generally did apply to contracts of employment, with a limitation applicable only to transportation workers.

The FAA, as a federal statute, is controlling both in federal and in state courts. Under the doctrine of "preemption," if an arbitration is governed by the FAA (essentially all contracts affecting interstate commerce), state courts must apply the FAA, even when a state statute might otherwise command a different result. Because of the preemptive effect of the FAA, for example, a state legislature cannot effectively prevent the enforcement of arbitration clauses merely because it had concluded that arbitration was not appropriate for certain classes of cases. Similarly, a state legislature may not declare that an arbitration agreement should not be enforced unless the agreement followed some special format. The FAA does not permit such limitations.

BASIC POLICY OF THE FAA

The FAA declares that a written provision authorizing arbitration (either prospectively, in a contract addressing other issues, but providing for arbitration of any disputes concerning such issues, or after-the-fact, in an agreement to submit an existing dispute to arbitration) shall be "valid, irrevocable, and enforceable, save upon such grounds as exist at law or in equity for the revocation of any contract." This simple statement wipes away decades of judicial hostility toward arbitration. In essence, the FAA makes an agreement to arbitrate as enforceable as any other contract.

There are limits on enforceability, however. The FAA provides that an agreement to arbitrate must be "written." That limitation has been interpreted broadly to include most forms of writings (formal contracts, but also exchanges of letters or telegrams, and agreements in which provisions for arbitration are incorporated by reference). Problems may arise, however, where an entity has not signed any agreement to arbitrate, but the entity has some relationship to a signatory (such as a parent or successor corporation, for example). In that event, the courts will generally apply ordinary contract law principles to determine whether the contract for arbitration is binding on the non-signatory.

Another limitation concerns grounds that would permit revocation of a contract. Thus, for example, a contract may be invalidated where it can be shown that a party entered the contract as a result of fraud. Broad allegations of fraudulent inducement of a contract, however, will generally not suffice to invalidate an arbitration agreement. A clause calling for arbitration and the larger agreement for a transaction (in which the arbitration clause may be buried) are considered separable contracts. A party seeking to defeat an arbitration agreement must show specifically that the provision for arbitration (not the larger contract, for whatever transaction occurred) was the product of fraud. Indeed, an arbitration may be conducted in which the very subject of the arbitration is whether the contract as a whole was the product of fraud.

Similar claims for invalidity of an arbitration clause may be launched on a host of other grounds: incapacity of a party (minors and legally incompetent people cannot form binding contracts), improper duress or coercion in forming the contract to arbitrate, or lack of consideration for the promise to arbitrate. Increasingly, especially with consumer contracts, there may be claims that the arbitration agreement was the product of "adhesion," or is "unconscionable," that is, that the agreement was presented on a take-it-or-leave-it basis, offered by a sophisticated party to an unsophisticated consumer, and with some other indications of unfairness (like lack of clear notice of the arbitration clause, or unfair procedures for the arbitration). Such challenges to an arbitration agreement may only be advanced, under the FAA, if the challenge could also be advanced against any other form of contract. In short, under the FAA, arbitration contracts are to be treated the same as other contracts. Special legal rules, aimed solely at invalidating arbitration contracts, are not proper.

Finally, the FAA contains a potential limitation requiring that the controversy to be arbitrated must "aris[e] out of" the contract that contains the arbitration clause. On a facial reading of the FAA, one might conclude that the FAA applies only to contract claims. In fact, courts have not imposed such a limitation. It is generally permissible to arbitrate claims that arise out of a contractual relationship even where the claims are based on statutory provisions, or other law that is not based on contract principles.

EFFECT ON PENDING LITIGATION

Where a matter is "referable to arbitration," and one of the parties to an arbitration agreement nevertheless brings an action in court, the FAA directs that the court shall "on application of one of the parties stay the trial of the action until such arbitration has been had in accordance with the terms of the agreement." Thus, the effect of the FAA is to permit a court to stay a pending action and direct parties to arbitrate in accordance with their agreement.

The power to stay, however, is not self-executing. One of the parties to the action must make an application to the court for a stay.

On such an application, the court may be required to test one or more of the issues in order to determine whether an arbitration agreement is binding. Is there no "written provision" to arbitrate? Is there ground for revocation of the agreement to arbitrate? If so, then the arbitration agreement may not be enforced.

There may also be grounds for a court to consider whether the subject matter involved in the arbitration proceeding is properly a matter for submission to arbitration. One issue in that regard is whether the arbitration clause is broad enough to cover the dispute submitted to arbitration. Generally, broad arbitration clauses (such as "any and all matters arising out of or relating to" the contract) will encompass almost all disputes, permitting arbitration. The parties, moreover, may specify in their arbitration agreement that the arbitrators (not the courts) should decide in the first instance whether a dispute is properly subject to arbitration. The notion is that an arbitrator has "jurisdiction to decide his own jurisdiction."

Another subject matter issue revolves around contentions that certain issues are not proper for arbitration under any circumstances as a matter of public policy. In the early years after the FAA was enacted, certain areas (such as matters arising under the securities laws) were considered improper subjects for arbitration. In more recent years, the courts (including the Supreme Court) have substantially restricted the categories of issues that are not properly subject to arbitration. Despite this trend in favor of arbitration, there is no black letter rule identifying all the categories of cases that are subject to arbitration.

In addition, there are circumstances when courts may hold that a party has waited too long to request a stay pending arbitration. Where a party has substantially participated in the litigation without requesting arbitration and the litigation has progressed to a substantial degree, a court may hold that the party has waived its right to pursue arbitration.

Finally, the FAA requires that the party seeking to stay litigation and pursue arbitration must not be in "default" in proceeding with the arbitration. Thus, for example, the arbitration provision, or applicable rules for the arbitration, may specify the time by which an arbitration demand must be lodged, arbitrators chosen, and proceedings commenced. If a party has ignored such time constraints, it may be held to have defaulted on its obligations to proceed with the arbitration.

COMPELLING ARBITRATION

The FAA provides that a party aggrieved by the "failure, neglect or refusal of another to arbitrate" may petition a court for an order directing that the arbitration proceed in the manner provided for in the parties' agreement. Thus, a court may issue an order directing parties to arbitrate even when there is no litigation pending. The party seeking to compel arbitration may commence an action by "petition" (similar to a complaint in litigation).

The FAA specifies that "[i]f the making of the arbitration agreement or the failure, neglect, or refusal to perform the same be in issue," the court must "proceed summarily to the trial thereof." Unless a jury trial is demanded, the judge will decide such issues. Using this procedure, a party may be able to gain a speedy resolution to the question of whether a counter-party to an arbitration agreement is, in fact, required to arbitrate.

The alternative is that the party seeking arbitration may commence an arbitration proceeding without knowing whether the arbitration agreement will ultimately be considered enforceable. A party might commence such an arbitration, and demand that the counter-party participate in the arbitration. Upon failure or refusal of the counter-party to participate, the initiating party might proceed to obtain a default award from an arbitrator. In a subsequent court proceeding to enforce the default award, the responding party might claim that it was not required to participate in the arbitration because there was no valid agreement to arbitrate. As a result, the initiating party would have gone through the expense and burden of arbitration proceedings for nothing.

The FAA cuts through that dilemma by permitting an initiating party to obtain an immediate direction compelling participation in the arbitration. The responding party, directed to participate in arbitration, may nevertheless choose not to participate, but it does so at great risk, because a claim that there was no valid arbitration agreement will have been resolved by the court's order compelling arbitration. Thus, a default arbitration award against a responding party that chooses not to participate in the arbitration may be quite effective.

APPOINTING ARBITRATORS

The FAA states that if the parties have, in their arbitration agreement, specified a method for choosing arbitrators, "such method shall be followed." If, however, no method is provided, or if the method provided fails, then a court may appoint the arbitrator or arbitrators. A court may similarly fill a vacancy on an arbitration panel, if no other method for filling the vacancy is available. The FAA also states that, "unless otherwise provided in the agreement," arbitrations shall be conducted by a single arbitrator.

In practice, the provisions of the FAA governing appointment of arbitrators are not often invoked. The method of selecting arbitrators is often specified in an agreement providing for arbitration. Further, the major arbitration-sponsoring institutions generally have very detailed procedures for selection of arbitrators. In the event that the parties have not specified a selection method in their agreement, typically the default procedures of the sponsoring institution will control. If no other methods are available, however, the ultimate stopgap is to resort to the courts.

DISPUTES TYPICALLY RESOLVED AS MOTIONS

The FAA states that any application to compel arbitration, to appoint an arbitrator, or to vacate or confirm an award shall be made and heard in the manner provided for the making and hearing of motions. No special pleading forms, or administrative procedures, are required. Typically, because the focus of an arbitration is a contractual provision (the agreement on arbitration), there is often little factual dispute about what contract governs, and what the contract says. Interpretation of a contract, moreover, is generally a matter for a court. Thus, it is often possible for a court to render summary judgment in favor of one party or another. If facts are in dispute, however, a trial may be required. The FAA recognizes the right of trial by jury in that event.

SUBPOENAS BY ARBITRATORS

The FAA provides that arbitrators may summon "any person to attend before them" as a witness, and "in a proper case" to bring with them "any book, record, document, or paper which may be deemed "material as evidence in the case." Such a "summons" is essentially a subpoena, but one that issues from the arbitrators, rather than from one of the parties. A summons is served in the same manner as a subpoena to appear and testify before a court.

A person summoned to testify before an arbitration tribunal who refuses or neglects to obey the summons may be subjected to an order of enforcement by a court. Such an order may be obtained by petition to the court in the district where the arbitrators are sitting to hear the case. Disobedience may also be punished by an order of contempt, in the same manner provided by law for punishment of neglect or refusal to attend as a witness in the court itself.

CONFIRMATION OF AN AWARD

An arbitration award is not self-executing. If the losing party does not comply with the award, the winning party may seek to "confirm" the award by having it entered as a judgment of a court. Once the award has been confirmed as a judgment, it may be enforced as if it had been rendered in an action in court, and in the manner by which any judgment is enforced (injunction, levy on property, garnishment of wages, etc.).

A motion to confirm an award must be filed within one year after the award is made. Such a motion may be made in any court that the parties have specified in their arbitration agreement. If the parties have not so specified, then the application may be made in the court in the district where the arbitration award was made. An award is generally "made" where it is issued by the arbitrators. The arbitrators will typically state, in the text of the award, where it was made. The institutional rules may also specify where an arbitration award is to be considered "made."

Notice of the motion to confirm an arbitration award must be served on the adverse party. The motion need contain nothing more than proof showing: (1) the arbitration agreement; (2) the selection of the arbitrators; (3) any specification of the time for making an award; and (4) the award. Once properly served, the motion must be granted, unless the adverse party shows grounds to vacate, modify or correct the award.

VACATING, MODIFYING OR CORRECTING AN AWARD

A motion to vacate, modify or correct an award may be made in opposition to a motion to confirm an award. Such a motion may also be made on its own. The FAA provides a short time frame for such a motion; a motion to vacate, modify or correct must be made within three months after the award is filed or delivered to the parties. In the event that a motion to vacate, modify or correct is made, a court may stay proceedings of an adverse party to enforce the award.

The FAA generally provides for review of arbitration awards only on narrow grounds. The few grounds stated in the FAA are: (1) the award was procured by "corruption, fraud, or undue means," (2) there was "evident partiality or corruption" in the arbitrators, (3) the arbitrators were guilty of "misconduct in refusing to postpone the hearing, on sufficient cause shown, or in refusing to hear evidence pertinent and material to the controversy," or of "any other misbehavior by which the rights of any party have been prejudiced," or (4) where the arbitrators have "exceeded their powers," or "so imperfectly executed them that a mutual, final, and definite award upon the subject matter submitted was not made." Adding to these statutory grounds, courts have sometimes suggested that, as a common law matter, arbitration awards may be vacated if they are "arbitrary and capricious" or they reflect "manifest disregard" for controlling law.

No matter how stated, however, these statutory and non-statutory factors generally operate on a presumption of correctness for arbitration awards, or at least an unwillingness on the part of courts to engage in searching review of such awards. It is often said that "mere error of fact or law" is not sufficient to vacate an arbitration award. Courts will generally not upset an award merely because they might reach a different decision than the arbitrators have reached.

This hesitation to engage in deep scrutiny of arbitration awards also follows from the practical problem that many arbitration decisions are essentially incapable of review. In many instances, the award does not contain any statement of reasons. A valid award need only state what issues have been decided, and what result is directed. The parties may request a reasoned decision, and some institutional rules provide for them, but reasoned decisions are not required in every case. So too, there is no universal rule that arbitration proceedings must be recorded by stenography or tape-recording. Thus, it is entirely possible that a reviewing court will have little more than an award and assertions of some problems in the arbitration process made by the losing party. Unless the reviewing court wishes to create an entirely new factual record (discovery, affidavits, testimony, etc.), the strong temptation may be to find no error.

Further, the worst forms of potential problems (such as "corruption" or "evident partiality") are not likely to occur in a well-administered arbitration. Most arbitration-sponsoring institutions, for example, have detailed systems for exposing conflicts of interest before an arbitration proceeds. Where parties have had the opportunity to raise objections to potential arbitrators, there is often a potent argument from waiver, where no such objections are made.

The difficulty in fashioning an appropriate remedy for problems in an arbitration also counsels against searching review. The FAA provides that, if an arbitration award is vacated, the court may direct a rehearing before the arbitrators who rendered the award. In the main, the FAA would permit a court to refer a case back to the original panel for reconsideration in light of the court's decision. But arbitrators are typically private citizens, who may not be available for continued service. In that event, if an award is vacated, the entire arbitration process (selection of a replacement arbitrator, and review of the prior proceedings, coupled with new proceedings to reconsider the award) may be quite cumbersome and expensive. Such practical concerns may also cause a court to hesitate in ordering an award vacated.

Nevertheless, even on the narrow standards for review outlined in the FAA, it is possible, in some instances, to obtain relief from an arbitration award. In essence, the FAA embodies a loose notion of "due process," in the sense of notice and an opportunity to be heard. If a party's due process rights have been egregiously violated, such that it has not been given a fair opportunity to present its case in arbitration, review may be had. Such cases are rare. Moreover, where a party has been given an opportunity to present its case, courts will almost never vacate an arbitration award merely because the arbitrators have ignored certain evidence, or found some pieces of evidence more important than others, or streamlined the arbitration process in a reasonable fashion.

The FAA also provides for limited review to modify or correct an award. Generally, an order modifying or correcting an award is designed to preserve the enforceability of an award that is valid but for some technical flaw. Thus, a court may modify or correct an award when: (1) there was an "evident material miscalculation of figures" or an "evident material mistake in the description of any person, thing, or property referred to in the award," (2) the arbitrators have "awarded upon a matter not submitted to them, unless it is a matter not affecting the merits of the decision," or (3) the award is "imperfect in matter of form not affecting the merits of the controversy." Such errors are generally apparent on the face of the award and unrelated to the merits of the dispute.

Courts are granted equitable powers to modify or correct an award to "effect the intent thereof and promote justice between the parties." Using this generous equitable power, courts may sever and confirm the portions of an award that are viable, and vacate, modify or correct the remainder of the award.

APPEAL

In 1988, the FAA was amended to specify the circumstances under which appeal could be taken from a court order concerning arbitration. In essence, Congress permitted appeal from "interlocutory" (or non-final) orders in arbitration cases, where such appeals would effectuate the congressional policy favoring implementation of arbitration agreements. Under the amended provisions, an appeal may be taken from any order (1) refusing to stay litigation pending arbitration, (2) denying a petition to compel arbitration, (3) denying confirmation of an arbitration award, (4) modifying, correcting or vacating an award, or (5) granting, continuing or modifying an injunction against an arbitration.

Appeal may also be taken from an order confirming an arbitration award, or from a "final decision" with respect to an arbitration. A decision is considered final where there is nothing more for the trial court to rule upon. The FAA specifies, however, that where a party has initiated an action on a matter that is otherwise referable to arbitration, and a court has stayed the action pending arbitration, the order staying the litigation is not final (and therefore not appealable). Similarly, where there is litigation on the merits and the district court directs arbitration, or at least refuses to enjoin arbitration, there is no immediate right of appeal.

The Uniform Arbitration Act

With few exceptions, most states have enacted some form of modern law on arbitration. The state statutes generally track the basic principles, and often the form, of the FAA. In 1955, the National Conference of Commissioners on Uniform State Laws adopted the Uniform Arbitration Act (UAA). The essential purpose of the UAA, like the FAA, was to eliminate traditional state law hostility toward arbitration, and to place arbitration agreements on the same footing as other contracts. The UAA is not binding in any jurisdiction, except to the extent that a particular state legislature has adopted it. In many instances, states have adopted the UAA wholesale, or with some exceptions or amendments. To understand a particular state's law, the specific arbitration statute adopted in that state must be reviewed.

Because the UAA post-dates the FAA by thirty years, it contains additional concepts that were not considered in the drafting of the FAA. It is useful to consider these added features because, to a large extent, they represent the trend in the development of arbitration law, which has, over time, increasingly supported extension of the use of arbitration.

FORMS OF HEARING AND DECISION

The UAA states that where more than one arbitrator serves on a tribunal, the powers of arbitrators are to be exercised by a majority, unless otherwise agreed. Hearings are to be conducted by all the arbitrators, except in circumstances where an arbitrator ceases to act. In that event, the remaining arbitrator or arbitrators may continue with the hearing and determination of the controversy.

The UAA specifies that at least five days' notice must be given to parties before an arbitration hearing is commenced, and that notice must be served personally, or by registered mail. If a party appears at a hearing, however, the requirements of notice are waived as to that party.

The UAA recognizes that arbitrators may hear and determine a controversy on evidence produced by one party where the other party has been duly notified of the hearing and has failed to appear.

The UAA provides that parties are entitled "to be heard, to present evidence material to the controversy and to cross-examine witnesses appearing at the hearing." The Act further states that a party has a right to be represented by an attorney, and that a waiver of this right prior to the proceeding or hearing is "ineffective."

The UAA grants arbitrators authority to issue subpoenas. It also states that, on application of a party for use as evidence, the arbitrators may permit a deposition to be taken of a witness who cannot be subpoenaed, or who cannot attend the hearing.

REVIEW OF AN AWARD

The UAA permits a party, within twenty days after an award is delivered, to apply to the arbitration tribunal to modify or correct the award. This power is generally limited to correction of mis-calculations, or revision of the form of the award, on grounds unrelated to the merits of the controversy. The UAA also permits arbitrators to change an award for purposes of "clarifying" it. When an application to amend or modify is made, the adverse party may serve objections. If the award is already the subject of an application to a court (to confirm or vacate the award), the court may direct that the arbitrators consider the request for modification or correction, under such conditions as the court may order.

The UAA states that, unless otherwise provided in the arbitration agreement, the arbitrators' expenses and fees, together with other expenses of the arbitration, are to be paid as provided in the award. Arbitrators may not award attorneys' fees unless specifical-ly authorized to do so by the arbitration agreement or by statute.

The UAA expressly recognizes that, in addition to other grounds, a party may seek to vacate an arbitration award because "there was no arbitration agreement." That ground may only be advanced if there has been no adverse determination on a prior proceeding to compel arbitration, and if the party aggrieved properly raised the objection before participating in the arbitra-tion hearing.

The UAA provides that a party must generally seek to vacate an adverse arbitration award within ninety days after it is delivered. If the purported ground is "corruption, fraud or other undue means" surrounding the award, however, the motion to vacate the award may be brought within ninety days after such grounds are known, "or should have been known."

The Revised Uniform Arbitration Act

In 2000, the National Conference of Commissioners on Uniform State Laws proposed the Revised Uniform Arbitration Act (RUAA). Several states are in the process of amending their arbitration laws to reflect the provisions of the RUAA. The text of the RUAA is well worth studying, because it represents the latest developments in the trend toward more sophisticated American arbitration law. To a large extent, the RUAA builds on the text of the FAA and the UAA. Fundamental principles of those statutory regimes have been preserved, and extended, in the RUAA.

NON-WAIVABLE ARBITRATION RIGHTS

The RUAA establishes three categories of requirements for the conduct of an arbitration proceeding. Generally, unless otherwise provided in the RUAA, parties may waive any of the requirements of the RUAA. This general provision operates from the basic principle of arbitration that parties should be free to structure an arbitration proceeding as they see fit, to meet their needs.

There are certain categories of requirements under the RUAA that may not be waived, "before a controversy arises." Presumably, after a controversy arises, parties will have a better idea of what their needs may be in the arbitration proceeding, and greater incentive to consider carefully any proposal for structuring the arbitration. The categories of requirements that may not be waived prospectively include: (1) the ability to apply for judicial relief in connection with the arbitration; (2) the enforceability of an arbitration agreement; (3) the ability to seek provisional relief from a court in connection with arbitration; (4) the ability to seek subpoenas and depositions of witnesses; (5) provisions on jurisdiction and appeal; (6) the requirement of reasonable notice on the commencement of an arbitration; (7) the requirement of reasonable disclosure of facts concerning potential bias of a neutral arbitrator; and (8) the right to be represented by a lawyer (except in labor arbitrations). These requirements may be waived after a controversy arises.

The RUAA also establishes a category of requirements that may never be waived. This category includes: (1) the general applicability of the RUAA, and the preservation of rights under the RUAA; (2) the ability to compel arbitration and to stay litigation; (3) the immunity of arbitrators; (4) the ability of an arbitrator to render a preliminary award; (5) the ability of an arbitrator to correct an award; and (5) the power of a court to confirm or vacate an award.

This identification of waivable and non-waivable requirements under the RUAA resolves a lingering question under the FAA and parallel state statutes. If arbitration is purely a creature of contract, then (in theory) any rights in arbitration may be waived or modified. The RUAA recognizes that certain requirements are so fundamental to due process, or so basic to our concept of how arbitration should proceed, that they cannot be waived, or at least cannot be waived prospectively.

VALIDITY OF AGREEMENT TO ARBITRATE

The RUAA, like the FAA and the UAA, recognizes the fundamental principle that an arbitration agreement is valid and enforceable, except on grounds that exist in law or equity to revoke a contract. The RUAA, however, specifies that a court, not an arbitrator, must decide whether an agreement to arbitrate exists, and whether a controversy is subject to an agreement to arbitrate. The RUAA also specifies that the arbitrator, not the court, shall decide whether a condition precedent to arbitrability has been fulfilled, and whether a contract containing a valid agreement to arbitrate is enforceable. Thus, the RUAA seeks to answer questions on the role and authority of the arbitrator and the court that may be left open under the FAA and the state statutory schemes.

The RUAA also makes clear that a challenge to the existence of a valid arbitration agreement should not delay arbitration proceedings. If such a challenge is made, "the arbitration proceeding may continue pending final resolution of the issue by the court," unless otherwise ordered.

PROVISIONAL REMEDIES

In keeping with common procedure in many states, the RUAA provides that before an arbitrator is appointed, a court may order provisional remedies designed to protect the effectiveness of the arbitration proceeding. Under that authority, for example, a court might take steps to preserve the status quo by preventing destruction or transfer of property that is the subject of the arbitration.

After an arbitrator is appointed, moreover, the RUAA grants the arbitrator specific authority to issue orders providing for provisional remedies. The RUAA permits an arbitrator to issue interim awards, which a party may seek to have enforced by a court on an expedited basis. A party may also seek assistance from a court if a matter is "urgent," and the arbitrator cannot provide a "timely" or "adequate" remedy. The RUAA specifies that a party does not waive its right to arbitration by seeking provisional remedies from a court.

CONSOLIDATION OF PROCEEDINGS

Ordinarily, because arbitration exists only by contractual agreement, parties to an individual arbitration agreement cannot be compelled to add one or more other parties to the arbitration proceedings, even if the other parties are related in some way to the matter at issue in the arbitration. For this reason, for example, there is generally no ability to conduct a class action by arbitration.

The RUAA, however, permits "consolidation" of separate arbitration proceedings, under certain limited circumstances. Under the

RUAA, a court may order consolidation as to some or all claims, so long as: (1) there are valid agreements to arbitrate; (2) the claims subject to arbitration arise "in substantial part" from the "same transaction or series of related transaction"; (3) the existence of a common issue of law or fact creates the possibility of conflicting decisions in the separate arbitration proceedings; and (4) the prejudice resulting from failure to consolidate is not outweighed by the risk of undue delay or prejudice to the rights of, or hardship to, any parties opposing consolidation.

The RUAA thus sets out a balancing test for consolidation. The RUAA specifies, however, that a court cannot order consolidation if an arbitration agreement specifically prohibits consolidation.

ARBITRATOR BIAS

The RUAA states that an individual who has a "known, direct and material interest" in the outcome of an arbitration proceeding or a "known, existing and substantial" relationship with a party may not serve as a "neutral," as opposed to party-appointed, arbitrator. Before accepting appointment, an arbitrator must make "reasonable inquiry" and disclose to all parties any known facts that a reasonable person would consider likely to affect the impartiality of the arbitrator, including a "financial or personal interest in the outcome," or an "existing or past relationship" with a party, counsel, witness or other arbitrator involved in the proceeding. An arbitrator also has a continuing obligation to disclose any such facts that the arbitrator learns after accepting appointment.

Under the RUAA, if an arbitrator discloses a fact concerning bias or interest, and a party timely objects, the arbitrator's continued service may be grounds for vacating an award. A neutral arbitrator who continues to serve in such circumstances is presumed to act with "evident partiality," such that an award may be vacated. Similarly, if such facts exist, and a neutral arbitrator fails to disclose them, an award presumptively must be vacated.

The RUAA recognizes, however, that the rules of any arbitration-sponsoring organization chosen by the parties must be followed. Substantial compliance with such procedures is a condition precedent to a motion to vacate an award on grounds of bias or interest of an arbitrator.

ARBITRATOR IMMUNITY

Consistent with the practice in most states and the rules of most arbitration-sponsoring organizations, the RUAA provides that an arbitrator or arbitration-sponsoring organization is immune from civil liability to the same extent as a judge. Arbitrators and representatives of arbitration-sponsoring organizations are not competent to testify, and may not be required to produce records, except to the extent that a judge might be required to do so, and to the extent necessary to resolve a claim by an arbitrator or arbitration-sponsoring organization against a party to an arbitration (e.g., for fees) or at a hearing on a motion to vacate an award, if the moving party establishes a *prima facie* ground for vacating the award.

The RUAA backs up the promise of arbitrator immunity with the potential for sanctions. If a person commences a civil action against an arbitrator or arbitration-sponsoring organization, and the court determines that arbitral immunity should be applied, the court must award reasonable attorney's fees and other reasonable expenses of litigation.

CONDUCTING AN ARBITRATION

The RUAA generally grants an arbitrator authority to conduct an arbitration in such manner as the arbitrator considers appropriate for a "fair and expeditious" disposition of the case. In particular, an arbitrator is permitted to conduct a "summary" proceeding if all parties agree, or on motion of one party if all other parties are given notice of the summary proceeding.

THE ARBITRATOR'S AWARD

Under the RUAA, an arbitrator may make pre-award rulings in favor of one party, which the party may ask the arbitrator to incorporate into an interim award. A party may move a court for an expedited order to confirm the award, and the court may summarily decide the motion.

More generally, after an award is issued, an arbitrator may, on motion of a party made within twenty days of the award, modify or correct the award. If a motion to confirm or vacate the award is already pending in court, the court may submit the request to modify or correct the award to the arbitrator.

The RUAA generally authorizes an arbitrator to award all remedies that the arbitrator considers "just and appropriate" under the circumstances. The fact that such remedy could not, or would not, be awarded by a court is not a ground for a court to refuse to confirm the award.

An arbitrator's expenses and fees, together with other expenses of the arbitration, must be paid as provided in the award. An arbitrator may also award reasonable attorney's fees and expenses if such an award is authorized by law, or by agreement of the parties.

An arbitrator may award punitive damages if such an award would be authorized by law in a civil action involving the same claim. If the arbitrator awards punitive damages, the arbitrator must specify in the award the basis in fact and law justifying and authorizing the award. The arbitrator must also identify the amount of punitive damages, as separate from any other damages in the award.

CONFIRMING OR VACATING AN AWARD

The RUAA generally provides that, on motion of a party, a court "shall" issue an order confirming an arbitration award, unless the award is vacated, modified or corrected. The potential grounds for vacating, modifying or correcting an award are generally the same as those recognized in the FAA and the UAA. The RUAA, however, specifies that if the ground for vacating an award pertains to the arbitrator's misconduct ("corruption, fraud or other undue means," "evident partiality of a neutral arbitrator" or "misconduct by an arbitrator prejudicing the rights of a party"), any rehearing of the matter must be conducted before a new arbitrator. Any other rehearing may be conducted before the arbitrator who made the award or that arbitrator's successor.

The RUAA permits a court to award reasonable costs for making a motion to confirm, vacate, modify or correct an award. If the motion is contested, the court may award the prevailing party its reasonable attorney's fees and expenses of litigation.

The RUAA generally provides that any court of the state that has jurisdiction over the parties and the controversy may enforce an agreement to arbitrate. The RUAA specifies that an agreement to arbitrate that provides for arbitration in a state automatically confers exclusive jurisdiction on the courts of that state to enter judgment on the award.

EFFECT OF THE RUAA

The RUAA is intended to serve as a state-of-the-art statutory framework for reforming arbitration laws. The RUAA, for example, expressly recognizes that a federal law on electronic signatures, adopted in 2000, applies to make effective electronic signatures on contracts for arbitration.

The RUAA, however, does not become effective in any state unless and until the particular state legislature adopts the statute. In adopting the RUAA, a legislature would generally repeal any existing arbitration law.

Regardless of whether a state legislature adopts the RUAA in whole or in part, to understand the arbitration law of a specific state, that state's individual arbitration statute must be reviewed in detail. Even if the RUAA does not become the uniform state law on arbitration that its framers envision, review of the Act is useful for its articulation of the most modern concepts of how arbitration law and proceedings should operate.

Chapter 3

THE AMERICAN ARBITRATION ASSOCIATION COMMERCIAL ARBITRATION RULES

The American Arbitration Association (AAA), a public service, not-for-profit organization headquartered in New York, is one of the largest providers of arbitration services in the world. For practitioners in the United States, basic familiarity with AAA procedures is essential. The AAA, moreover, aims to provide state-of-the-art procedures for arbitration. An understanding of AAA procedures provides a good grounding for comparison of arbitration procedures offered by other arbitration-sponsoring institutions, and for the construction of *ad hoc* procedures that may incorporate many of the procedures established by the AAA.

Arbitration Clause

The AAA Commercial Arbitration Rules (the Rules), which may be found in their entirety on the World Wide Web at www.adr.org/rules/commercial, recommend that parties who wish to provide for AAA arbitration insert a specific clause in their contracts:

> *Any controversy or claim arising out of or relating to this contract, or the breach thereof, shall be settled by arbitra-*

tion administered by the American Arbitration Association under its Commercial Arbitration Rules, and judgment on the award rendered by the arbitrator(s) may be entered in any court having jurisdiction thereof.

Even when the parties have not previously provided for arbitration of disputes under their contract, they may agree to submit an existing dispute to arbitration. The AAA recommends the following form of submission agreement:

We, the undersigned parties, hereby agree to submit to arbitration administered by the American Arbitration Association under its Commercial Arbitration Rules the following controversy: (describe briefly). We further agree that the above controversy be submitted to (one) (three) arbitrator(s). We further agree that we will abide by and perform any award rendered by the arbitrator(s), and that a judgment of any court having jurisdiction may be entered on the award.

In addition to rules governing commercial disputes, the AAA offers special rules for labor disputes and for arbitration of disputes in particular industries, such as telecommunications. Whenever parties provide for arbitration before the AAA without specifying particular rules, they will generally be deemed to have chosen the Commercial Rules for their arbitration. If the parties wish to use other governing rules, they should specify their choice.

Similarly, if the parties merely wish to "borrow" the AAA rules for an *ad hoc* arbitration (not administered by the AAA) they should specify that choice. The Rules provide that, when parties agree to arbitrate under the AAA Rules, they "thereby authorize the AAA to administer the arbitration," unless the parties otherwise specifically provide.

Sources of Rules for Arbitration

The AAA generally recognizes that the parties, "by written agreement," may vary any of the procedures in the Rules. As a result, the ultimate source of rules for an AAA arbitration is the parties themselves. If the parties have agreed to a specific procedure in their arbitration contract or submission agreement, that procedure controls. Further, the parties may, during the course of the arbitration, agree on procedures that omit, amend or add to the procedures set out in the AAA Rules.

The AAA Rules are updated from time to time. Unless the parties agree otherwise, the most current form of the Rules in effect at the time that the arbitration is initiated will be applied by the AAA.

Generally, under the Rules, once an arbitrator is appointed, the arbitrator has authority to "interpret and apply" the Rules, as they relate to the arbitrator's powers and duties. In particular, the arbitrator has the power to rule on "his or her own jurisdiction, including any objections with respect to the existence, scope or validity of the arbitration agreement." Similarly, the arbitrator sets the date, time and place for any arbitration hearing, and may exercise "discretion" in conducting the proceedings, with "a view to expediting the resolution of the dispute." When there is more than one arbitrator, differences concerning the application of the Rules are decided by majority vote.

The AAA generally interprets and applies all "other" rules concerning the administration of the arbitration (e.g., the selection of arbitrators, submission of pleadings, and payment of fees). The AAA assigns a case administrator to each case. The administrator is affiliated with a particular office of the AAA. The AAA may assign administration to any of its offices. The administrator is generally responsible for coordinating any communication with the arbitrators, unless the parties have otherwise agreed. Parties are permitted, however, to have *ex parte* discussions with their own party-appointed arbitrator.

Generally, when the AAA or the arbitrator has made an error in administering an arbitration, a written objection should be lodged as soon as possible. The AAA Rules provide that a party who fails to object "shall be deemed to have waived the right to object." Many individual AAA Rules, moreover, call for prompt objection, on pain of waiver. For example, a party who objects to the jurisdiction of an arbitrator, or arbitrability of claim, must state the objection in that party's initial pleading.

Pleadings

When an arbitration is commenced pursuant to a contract, the initiating party (the claimant) must provide the responding party (the respondent) with notice of intention to arbitrate (a demand for arbitration). The demand for arbitration may be quite brief, setting forth no more than the nature of the dispute (e.g., breach of contract), the names and addresses of all other parties, the amount involved, the remedy sought, and the requested hearing locale. The AAA form for demand of arbitration is a single page in length. The demand is filed with the AAA, together with a filing fee, and the AAA confirms notice of the demand to the responding parties. The demand for arbitration may be more elaborate, but it must, when filed, be accompanied by a copy of the arbitration provision (or provisions) pursuant to which the arbitration is authorized.

The respondent may file an answering statement, within fifteen days after the AAA confirms the notice of demand for arbitration. Again, the answering statement need not be complex. Indeed, if the respondent does not file an answering statement, the respondent will be deemed to have generally denied the claim. Any objections to jurisdiction or arbitrability, however, must be expressly stated. If the respondent's answering statement includes a counterclaim, moreover, it must contain the same kind of information as required in a demand for arbitration, and must be accompanied by the appropriate fee.

The Rules suggest that parties should provide descriptions of their claims in sufficient detail to "make the circumstances of the dispute clear to the arbitrator." Many practitioners, accustomed to civil procedure rules, file more elaborate pleadings, with numbered paragraphs, separate claims for relief, and other formal pleading flourishes.

The Rules also permit parties to amend their claims at any time before an arbitrator is appointed. After appointment of an arbitrator, consent of the arbitrator is required before filing a new pleading.

The arbitrator is authorized to require the parties to clarify the issues and claims in the case. This may be done orally, at a preliminary conference. If the claim or counterclaim is worth at least $1 million, the AAA will apply its Optional Procedures for Large, Complex Commercial Disputes (Large Case Procedures). The Large Case Procedures permit the arbitrator to direct the parties to submit "detailed" statements of claims and legal authorities, stipulations of uncontested facts, and other aids to the efficient conduct of proceedings. Similar procedures may be used in smaller cases, when appropriate.

Frequently, after arbitration hearings are complete in a case, the parties will submit post-hearing briefs. The arbitrator, on his or her own initiative, may require such briefs, as a method of summarizing the evidence, issues and law applicable to the case.

Mediation

In addition to administering arbitrations, the AAA also offers mediation services. The AAA charges no additional administrative fee where parties to a pending arbitration attempt to mediate their dispute under the auspices of the AAA.

The AAA Commercial Mediation Rules (Mediation Rules) require a written contract or stipulation for submission to mediation. As with arbitration, the AAA offers model forms of mediation clauses.

Once a request for mediation (with brief statement of the nature of the dispute) has been filed, the AAA will appoint a mediator, either from its list of neutrals, or as agreed between the parties. There is a procedure for disclosure of conflicts, objections by the parties, and filling of any vacancies in the appointment of the mediator.

The mediator sets dates and times for mediation sessions. Before the first session, the parties provide the mediator with brief memoranda concerning the dispute. The mediator may direct that the memoranda be exchanged between the parties. The mediator may also require production of information required for the mediator to understand the issues, and may seek expert assistance where necessary.

The mediator cannot impose a settlement, but will attempt to help the parties reach a satisfactory resolution of their dispute. The mediator may conduct separate and/or joint meetings. The mediator may end the mediation sessions when it appears that further sessions would not be productive. Any party may also declare that the proceedings should be terminated.

All mediation sessions are private. Any confidential information provided to the mediator cannot be disclosed. Views expressed, and proposals made, during mediation sessions are treated as settlement discussions, not to be used as evidence in other proceedings. No stenographic records are kept of mediation sessions.

The AAA claims a very high rate of success from use of its mediation processes. When mediation fails to achieve a settlement of the dispute, the mediator ordinarily performs no further function. The parties may, by consent, permit the mediator to continue to serve, but in the role of an arbitrator, rather than as mediator.

Selection of an Arbitrator

The Commercial Rules generally distinguish between a party-appointed arbitrator, and a "neutral" arbitrator. A party-appointed arbitrator is not subject to disqualification for bias or prior relationship with a party. A neutral arbitrator is. Typically, when the arbitrator appointment process includes party-appointed arbitrators, each party will appoint one arbitrator, and the two party-appointed arbitrators will choose the third, neutral arbitrator, who will serve as chair of the arbitration tribunal.

Generally, if the parties have specified a method for selection of arbitrator(s), the AAA will follow that method. If the parties have not specified a method of selection, or the chosen method fails, the AAA procedures will be used.

Most often, the AAA method for appointment of an arbitrator is to send each party an identical list of names of persons who could serve as arbitrator. The parties may agree to designate an arbitrator from this list. If they do not agree on an arbitrator, they are given a number of days to return the list to the AAA, striking a fixed number of names from the list, and ranking the remaining names in preferred order. The AAA will choose the highest-ranked arbitrator who is mutually agreeable to the parties. If this selection method fails, or if the arbitration involves three or more parties, the AAA will appoint the arbitrator directly.

If the arbitration agreement sets a period of time for the parties to designate their party-appointed arbitrators, or for the party-appointed arbitrators to select the neutral arbitrator, that time period will be enforced. Otherwise, the Rules set a period for such appointment (generally fifteen days). If the period lapses, the AAA will make the appointment.

If the arbitration agreement does not specify the number of arbitrators, the arbitration will ordinarily be conducted by a single arbitrator. For smaller cases (worth less than $75,000) the AAA Expedited Procedures mandate that there will be only one arbitrator. For large cases (worth more than $1 million) the Large Case Procedures generally require that there be three arbitrators.

The AAA Rules do not generally impose restrictions on the qualifications for arbitrators. An arbitrator need not be a lawyer, for example. When the parties are nationals of different countries, however, the AAA at the request of any party or on its own initiative will appoint a neutral arbitrator from a country other than the countries of the parties.

Once an arbitrator candidate has been chosen, the AAA will send notice to the candidate, who must indicate acceptance of the appointment in writing. The candidate must also disclose to the AAA any circumstances "likely to affect impartiality or independence" of a neutral arbitrator, including "any bias or any financial interest in the result of the arbitration or any past or present relationship with the parties or their representatives." The AAA provides this information to the parties, who may object. AAA decisions on any such objections are "conclusive." Upon disqualification of the chosen arbitrator, the AAA may either repeat the prior procedure used to select the neutral arbitrator, or may simply appoint a replacement arbitrator itself.

Initial Proceedings

Even before an arbitrator is selected, the AAA administrator may conduct an initial administrative conference (in person, or by telephone) to discuss such matters as arbitrator selection, potential mediation, exchange of information, a timetable for hearings and other relevant matters. The AAA may also determine the locale for the arbitration, if the parties have not otherwise agreed. No administrative conferences are held in expedited (small) cases. Such conferences are mandated, however, in large cases.

Once the arbitrator is appointed and the case is ready to proceed, the arbitrator may conduct a preliminary hearing, in person or by telephone. A preliminary hearing may address any number of issues, including discovery, methods to clarify and narrow the issues, and the schedule for hearings.

The expedited procedures for small cases do not provide for a preliminary hearing. Instead, the procedures contemplate that a single hearing, generally lasting no more than one day, will be used to submit proof. For very small cases ($10,000 or less) the matter will be decided on submission of documents, with no oral hearing unless one of the parties specifically requests it, or the arbitrator so directs.

For large, complex matters, a preliminary hearing must be conducted, "as soon as practicable" after the arbitrator is appointed. The preliminary hearing may address a wide array of issues:

(a) service of a detailed statement of claims, damages and defenses, a statement of the issues asserted by each party and positions with respect thereto, and any legal authorities the parties may wish to bring to the attention of the arbitrators; (b) stipulations to contested facts; (c) the extent to which discovery shall be conducted; (d) exchange and premarking of those documents which each party believes may be offered at the hearing; (e) the identification and availability of witnesses, including experts, and such matters with respect to witnesses including their biographies

*and expected testimony as may be appropriate;
(f) whether, and the extent to which, any sworn statements
and/or depositions may be introduced; (g) the extent to
which hearings will proceed on consecutive days;
(h) whether a stenographic or other official record of the
proceedings shall be maintained; and (i) the possibility of
utilizing mediation or other non-adjudicative methods of
dispute resolution.*

The AAA Large Case Procedures state that even this laundry list of topics for consideration at a preliminary hearing is "without limitation" to other issues.

Discovery and Evidence

The Commercial Rules do not follow the standards of codes of civil procedure or evidence to which most practitioners are accustomed. On discovery, for example, the Rules merely provide that an arbitrator, at the request of a party, "may direct" the production of documents and other information, and the identification of witnesses to be called. Such discovery may include subpoenas to non-parties, at the direction of the arbitrator. The Rules also permit an arbitrator to conduct an "inspection or investigation" as part of the information-gathering process, when "necessary." At least five days before any evidentiary hearing, the parties must exchange copies of the exhibits they intend to submit.

The expedited procedures for small cases do not contemplate any discovery. Instead, the procedures merely require exchange of exhibits, at least two days before the evidentiary hearing. For a large, complex case, the procedures expressly contemplate more extensive discovery, so long as it is "consistent with the goal of achieving a just, speedy and cost-effective resolution" of the case.

Thus, the parties are expected to agree on the extent of document discovery. If they cannot, the arbitrator will establish guidelines. Similarly, "for good cause shown," the arbitrator may order depositions of, or the propounding of interrogatories to, persons who may possess information "necessary" to the determination of the case.

As with discovery, the AAA procedures contemplate relaxed rules of evidence for the purpose of ruling on factual issues in arbitration. The Rules expressly state that "[c]onformity to legal rules of evidence shall not be necessary." Nevertheless, the arbitrator retains broad discretion to determine the admissibility, relevance and materiality of evidence, and may exclude evidence deemed to be cumulative or irrelevant. The arbitrator is also required to take privilege issues into account, including (in particular) the privilege for attorney/client communications.

The AAA Rules expressly contemplate submission of testimony by declaration or affidavit, without a right of cross-examination. If this method of submission is used, the arbitrator may consider objections to proffered testimony, and may give the testimony "only such weight" as appears appropriate in light of such evidence. Indeed, it is common in AAA arbitrations for an arbitrator to admit many forms of evidence (not just declarations or affidavits) subject to objections, such as hearsay or lack of foundation. Arbitrators will often state, in such circumstances, that the evidence will be considered only "for what it's worth."

The Conduct of Hearings

The parties are always permitted to waive oral hearings. Ordinarily, when a hearing is requested, the claimant presents evidence first, with the respondent subsequently presenting its case. Witnesses are subject to cross-examination, and may also be questioned by the arbitrator. The arbitrator is permitted to bifurcate hearings, or to otherwise order the proof to expedite resolution of the case.

Hearings need not be conducted on consecutive days. For large, complex cases, however, the arbitrator may consider setting aside several consecutive days to conduct the hearing. For small cases, the presumption is that the hearing will be conducted in a single day.

Although the arbitrator sets the dates, times and place for any hearing, all parties must be given notice of the hearing. Parties are entitled to be represented by counsel or another authorized representative. An arbitrator may postpone a hearing on agreement of the parties, or "for good cause shown."

Hearings are private. Any person with a direct interest in the case may attend. Witnesses may be excluded during the testimony of other witnesses. Any party may, at its own expense, provide for a stenographic record of hearings. Similarly, any party that requires an interpreter must make arrangements for, and pay for, such services. In small cases, generally there will be no stenographic record.

After due notice, an arbitration hearing may proceed in the absence of a party, or its representative. An award, however, cannot be made solely on the default of a party. The party seeking an award on default must present some evidence, as directed by the arbitrator.

The arbitrator must inquire of the parties before closing the hearing. The arbitrator may receive post-hearing briefs from the parties. At any time before the award, the arbitrator may reopen the hearing to permit submission of additional evidence.

The Award

An arbitrator may enter an interim award, including injunctive relief and measures for the protection or conservation of property and disposition of perishable goods. The AAA also offers Optional Rules for Emergency Measures of Protection, to which the parties may agree. More generally, an arbitrator may grant any remedy that the arbitrator deems to be "just and equitable," within the scope of the arbitration agreement. An award may include interest and attorney's fees, so long as such fees are authorized by the parties' agreement, or by law.

The arbitrator must make the award "promptly," generally no more than thirty days from the date of closing of the hearing and the conclusion of any post-hearing briefing. The award must be in writing, but it need not contain reasons for the award, unless the parties request a reasoned award, or the arbitrator determines that a reasoned award is appropriate. Once an award is rendered, any party may request, through the AAA, that clerical, typographical or computational errors be corrected. The arbitrator may not redetermine the merits of any claim already decided.

Court Proceedings

On request of a party, the AAA will provide certified copies of any appropriate records for use in judicial proceedings. The Rules provide, however, that neither the AAA nor any arbitrator should be a necessary party in any judicial proceedings related to an arbitration. The Rules also contemplate that the AAA and any arbitrator will enjoy immunity from liability for "any act or omission" in connection with any arbitration.

Fees, Expenses and
Arbitrator Compensation

In the event of extreme hardship, the AAA may defer or reduce its administrative fees. Generally, the AAA charges a filing fee, keyed to the amount of the claim or counterclaim, a hearing fee for each day of hearing held, a postponement or cancellation fee (where a party has caused the postponement or cancellation), and a hearing room rental fee. The hearing room fee does not apply when hearings are held at locations other than AAA offices. There is also no hearing fee for the initial AAA administrative hearing.

All other expenses, including travel and other expenses of witnesses and the arbitrator, are to be borne equally by the parties, unless they have otherwise agreed, or unless the arbitrator assesses expenses against one of the parties. The compensation of a party-appointed arbitrator is arranged directly between the party and the arbitrator. The compensation of a neutral arbitrator is arranged through the AAA, at the neutral arbitrator's stated rate. For claims under $10,000, the arbitrator customarily serves without compensation.

If arbitrator compensation or administrative fees are not paid, the AAA may so inform the parties, and the arbitrator or the AAA may suspend or terminate the proceedings. The AAA may also require that the parties deposit sums in advance of the hearings, to cover fees and expenses.

FUNDAMENTAL
LEGAL CONCEPTS

The Contractual Nature
of Arbitration

At its core, the legitimacy of arbitration depends on the agreement of the parties to a dispute. As we have seen, in the period preceding the adoption of the FAA and related statutes, there was some question whether parties could, by contract, choose arbitration to the exclusion of judicial processes for dispute resolution. The modern view (backed by the FAA and related state statutes) is that arbitration contracts are as effective and binding as other types of contracts.

The often-stated observation that "arbitration is a creature of contract," however, is pregnant with legal issues, many of which are still being played out in the courts. The principle of party autonomy in forming arbitration contracts generally aims to permit parties to choose the form of arbitration, and character of arbitrators, that best suit their needs. That principle, however, has some obvious limits (parties could not, for example, choose some illegal form of arbitration, like trial by combat). Even within these obvious limits, moreover, public policy concerns have often affected the law of arbitration.

The Principle of Separability

Courts often refer to arbitration clauses as special forms of forum selection agreements. Just as a contract might provide that, in the event of a dispute arising out of the contract, the parties agree to litigate in a particular judicial forum, parties may similarly choose arbitration as the forum for dispute resolution. In essence, the parties have made two separate contracts: one governing the substance of their relationship, and the other providing for the forum for dispute resolution.

The separability of these two contracts is important in cases in which a party claims that the main contract is void on one or more grounds. If a party could, simply by alleging that a contract was void (for fraud, duress, etc.), evade the arbitration agreement, then the effectiveness of such arbitration agreements might be jeopardized. Courts might be tempted to interfere in the arbitration process (to test the validity of such claims), and even if courts did not interfere at the outset of the process, arbitration might proceed at the risk that, ultimately, the results of an arbitration proceeding could be voided on such grounds.

In response to these kinds of concerns, courts have erected substantial barriers to any attempt to void an arbitration clause in a contract. The principle of separability of the main contract and the arbitration contract has been interpreted to mean that, even if a party claims that a substantive contract is void, the separate arbitration provision is not void unless the party can show specifically that the arbitration provision itself was the product of fraud, duress or other factors sufficient to void the arbitration agreement. This standard, in practice, is generally quite difficult to meet. As a result, it is entirely possible to have a binding arbitration agreement, even when one of the central issues in the case is whether the substantive contract at issue is void.

Scope of Submission
to Arbitration

Just as parties generally enjoy freedom to choose the arbitration process that best suits their needs, so too do they enjoy the freedom to choose which matters they will submit to arbitration. In a dispute involving real estate, for example, parties might choose to employ an expert appraiser to arbitrate the question of the value of the real estate. Other questions in dispute (such as liability under a contract), however, might be reserved for decision by judge or jury (or even, conceivably, a different arbitrator). The point is that, because arbitration is a procedure that depends on the consent of the parties, if parties have chosen to arbitrate some, but not all, matters in dispute, that choice must be respected.

Indeed, the principle of party autonomy and respect for the contractual nature of arbitration means that parties cannot be compelled to arbitrate where they have not agreed to do so even though partial arbitration may produce duplicative, inefficient dispute resolution. Although it is often stated that the goal of arbitration is speedy, cheap dispute resolution, acceptance of that goal cannot be forced upon litigants. Party autonomy generally trumps efficiency as a factor in interpreting and enforcing an arbitration agreement.

Contractual Inarbitrability

Generally, when a matter is not capable of being arbitrated, it is referred to as "inarbitrable." The concept of inarbitrability, however, has many facets. One broad category of inarbitrability problems relates to the validity of the contract for arbitration. As noted, a party may challenge the arbitration contract as the product of fraud, duress or on other grounds for voiding the contract. Further, as noted, a party may assert that the terms of the arbitration agreement do not include specific claims or issues.

There may be other problems with the arbitration agreement, however. For example, the requirement under the FAA and related statutes is that any arbitration agreement be stated in writing. This requirement has been interpreted broadly to permit arbitration based on the exchange of correspondence referring to arbitration, and other similar situations in which there may not be a single arbitration agreement signed by the party who later resists arbitration. In essence, the writing requirement may be satisfied by some written evidence that the parties have agreed to arbitrate, so long as it is possible to determine from that evidence that there has been a definite agreement to arbitrate. Nevertheless, under the FAA and related statutes, an agreement to arbitrate cannot be evidenced solely by oral testimony.

Similar problems arise where a non-signatory to an arbitration agreement is involved. In such a circumstance, there is no written agreement to arbitrate involving the non-signatory (although there may be an agreement among other parties), and the non-signatory ordinarily cannot be bound to an arbitration process to which it has not agreed. Exceptions to this rule may be found in general contract principles, such as the doctrine of incorporation by reference. Thus, where one contract contains no arbitration provision, but incorporates, by reference, another contract containing an arbitration provision, arbitration may be conducted even though a party did not sign the actual contract containing the arbitration provision. Various other theories (piercing the corporate veil, successorship, principal and agent, etc.) have also been used, on occasion, to compel a non-signatory to arbitrate.

Moreover, a non-signatory to an arbitration agreement may not intervene in an arbitration proceeding, absent consent of the other parties. For this reason, a class action procedure is virtually impossible in the context of arbitration. Similarly, the barrier against arbitration with non-signatories will often preclude third-party practice. Although arbitration involving the main parties may proceed, if the respondent believes that a non-signatory third party is also responsible in some way, the non-signatory cannot be compelled to participate in the arbitration. Litigation against the non-signatory third party may proceed at the same time as the arbitration, or may await the outcome of the arbitration. Again, even though class action, intervention and third-party practice might be considered desirable and efficient, the contractual nature of the authority for arbitration generally precludes arbitration absent the consent of all the parties.

Substantive Inarbitrability and
Public Policy Limits on Arbitration

In the earliest history of arbitration, courts were highly skeptical of the ability of arbitrators to perform the dispute resolution functions that the courts so jealously guarded. As a result, until the passage of the FAA and related state statutes, the common law rule was generally to the effect that arbitration agreements were voidable at the option of any party.

The passage of the FAA and related state statutes, however, did not completely reverse the judicial antipathy to arbitration. Indeed, in a series of decisions, the Supreme Court of the United States repeatedly suggested that certain types of disputes were incapable of proper resolution through arbitration. In *Wilko v. Swan,* 346 U.S. 427, 74 S.Ct. 182, 98 L.Ed. 168 (1953), for example, the Court held that the effectiveness of the federal securities laws could be impaired if parties were permitted to consent to arbitration of securities law claims, to the exclusion of the courts. Courts followed, and extended, that public policy limitation on arbitration for years thereafter.

By the early 1980s, however, the Supreme Court had recognized a "liberal federal policy" favoring arbitration, embodied in the FAA. See *Moses H. Cone Memorial Hospital v. Mercury Construction Corporation,* 460 U.S. 1, 103 S.Ct. 927, 74 L.Ed.2d 765 (1983). Thereafter, the Court, in a series of decisions, declared that public policy did not preclude arbitration involving important federal rights, including rights under the RICO statute, the antitrust laws and, ultimately, rights under the securities laws. Thus, the *Wilko v. Swan* public policy inarbitrability limit has virtually disappeared.

What remains of the public policy-based inarbitrability doctrine essentially relates to forms of judicial decision-making that are truly public in character. Thus, criminal cases, which involve a public prosecutor representing the public interest, are almost certainly not capable of arbitration. More difficult intermediate cases imbued with at least a partial public interest include matters of child custody and bankruptcy. The law in this area is evolving, and the precise contours of the remaining substantive inarbitrability doctrine will likely be mapped in years to come.

Who Decides Issues of Arbitrability?

The traditional formulation of the rule on who decides whether a matter is inarbitrable is that "an arbitrator has jurisdiction to decide his (or her) own jurisdiction." Under that view, where a party challenges arbitration proceedings on inarbitrability grounds, the arbitrator may rule, in the first instance, on the challenge and proceed with the arbitration based on that ruling. After the award is rendered, a party may challenge the award by claiming, among other things, that the arbitrator exceeded his or her powers in some way. In that manner, the arbitrator, and ultimately the courts, may both review contractual and substantive inarbitrability issues.

Despite that traditional view of an arbitrator's "competence to decide his or her own competence," the dynamics of arbitration do not always lend themselves to an arbitrator first, courts later, sequence of review. If a party claims that it is not a proper party to an arbitration (because it has not signed an arbitration agreement, because it was defrauded into agreeing to arbitration, or because it claims that the subject matter is incapable of arbitration), it may simply refuse to participate in the arbitration. The claimant may pursue an award by default, with the possibility that the defaulting party will prevail on judicial review of the default award (by showing that the award was improperly obtained).

That default review process can be quite inefficient and involves significant risk of wasted effort. The FAA thus permits a party to move to compel participation in the arbitration. In that context, inarbitrability issues may be presented immediately to a court for review. Where such issues are presented, and a court nevertheless orders arbitration to proceed, a party cannot simply refuse to respond in the arbitration proceeding and expect to be able to present its inarbitrability challenges to a court later.

Further, although the language of the FAA does not specifically countenance this procedure, courts have suggested that, in the same way that a party may move to compel arbitration where a valid arbitration agreement exists, a party may also move to preclude arbitration where no valid arbitration agreement exists. Thus, again, inarbitrability issues may be addressed even before an arbitrator has ruled on his or her own jurisdiction.

The Supreme Court gave a great boost to parties attempting to attain immediate judicial review in *First Options of Chicago, Inc. v. Kaplan,* 514 U.S. 938, 115 S.Ct. 1920, 131 L.Ed.2d 992 (1995). The Court held that, just as parties may choose what substantive issues they wish to submit to arbitration, so too they may choose whether they wish a court, or an arbitrator, to determine the arbitrability of any claims in arbitration. Further, the Court held that there is no presumption that an arbitrator will decide all issues of arbitrability. Instead, unless parties have clearly expressed a desire to have an arbitrator decide arbitrability issues, courts are free to make their own independent decisions on arbitrability.

The practical consequence of a decision on who should decide arbitrability (an arbitrator or a court) is more than a matter of timing. Under the FAA and related state statutes, if a matter is arbitrable, and a valid arbitration agreement exists, then the choice of arbitration precludes resort to the courts. An action in court based on the arbitrable claim is not permitted. Further, upon entry of an award by the arbitrator, any review of the award in a court is quite limited. Thus, the conclusion that the arbitrator, rather than the court should, in the first instance, decide the issue of the arbitrator's jurisdiction may have great significance.

What Law Applies to the Implementation of an Arbitration Agreement?

Parties to a contract of arbitration (or an arbitration clause in a larger contract) will often choose the substantive state law that is meant to govern their contract. In interpreting the contract, the arbitrator will generally adhere to that choice of law. But what of the choice of law (between the Federal Arbitration Act and state statutes) when a court interprets and implements an arbitration agreement? What if the state statute is inconsistent with the FAA, or contains a provision that the FAA does not itself authorize?

It is important to note that, for domestic matters (internal to the United States), the FAA does not provide an automatic grant of jurisdiction to the federal courts. (There is an automatic grant of federal court subject matter jurisdiction in international arbitration cases.) In domestic cases, if a dispute is purely between parties from the same state and does not otherwise raise federal claims, there generally will be no basis for resort to the federal courts. Any judicial supervision of the arbitration process will thus take place in the state court. In such instances, moreover, where it cannot be shown that the dispute involves "commerce" among the states, the FAA's substantive terms would not apply to a purely intrastate dispute. The state court would apply the provisions of the applicable state statute on arbitration.

The concept of "interstate commerce" is interpreted broadly, however, and the category of purely intrastate cases is thus relatively small. Where the interstate commerce element is present, the FAA governs, even if the dispute is in state, not federal, court. The FAA is the "supreme law of the land," and generally preempts contrary state law.

The breadth of preemption by the FAA, however, remains a matter of considerable debate. In *Southland Corp. v. Keating,* 465 U.S. 1, 104 S.Ct. 852, 79 L.Ed.2d 1 (1984), for example, the Supreme Court held that a California franchise investment statute, which declared that claims under the state statute could be considered only by a court (thus precluding arbitration), was preempted by the FAA. The state law, the Court declared, frustrated the purpose of the FAA, to place arbitration agreements upon the same footing as other contracts. Because the state franchise investment law would void certain categories of arbitration agreements, the law was preempted by the FAA.

By contrast, in *Volt Information Sciences, Inc. v. Stanford University,* 489 U.S. 468, 109 S.Ct. 1248, 103 L.Ed.2d 488 (1989), the Court held that a California arbitration statute, which permitted a court to stay arbitration proceedings pending resolution of related litigation, was not preempted by the FAA. The Court held that, by choosing California law to govern their arbitration agreement, the parties had chosen the California arbitration statute's procedures. Thus, enforcing the arbitration agreement (as required by the FAA) was not inconsistent with following the state arbitration procedure that the parties had chosen.

The rule thus appears to be that a state cannot invalidate all, or a whole category of, arbitration agreements (in violation of the FAA), but may adopt provisions to govern arbitration, which parties may choose to implement in their arbitration agreements. Yet, this simple formulation of the preemption rule does not answer all preemption questions. For example, the FAA provides for only limited judicial review of an arbitration award. Courts have held, however, that parties are free to adopt procedures for stricter review of an award in their arbitration agreements. Even though such stricter review of arbitration awards is not authorized by the FAA, if the parties choose such stricter review, the FAA is not violated. In the same way, if a state legislature adopted a procedural statute governing arbitration, and parties chose to subject themselves to the statute by choosing the state's law to govern their agreement, questions would arise concerning whether the state procedure was inconsistent with the FAA and whether the parties could choose to waive, or opt out, of the FAA. These precise questions, and many variations on them, will likely be addressed by the courts in years to come.

What Law Must an Arbitrator Apply?

Arbitrators are private actors who will resolve a dispute and then move on to other, unrelated activities. Arbitration proceedings, moreover, are generally private matters. Even if an arbitration award contains a statement of reasons for the award, that statement is generally not publicized, and the results of one arbitration are generally not considered of precedential value in another arbitration. Strictly speaking, therefore, there is no "law of arbitration" for arbitrators to apply. Instead, in rendering a decision, an arbitrator will generally attempt to follow the law of the jurisdiction chosen by the parties or, absent a clear choice by the parties, will attempt to discern the parties' intent as to choice of law from other factors surrounding the making and implementation of the contract. On procedural matters (such as the issuance of subpoenas to third-party witnesses), the arbitrator will generally follow the law of the jurisdiction in which the arbitration is conducted.

In the international arbitration context, there are some commentators who suggest that an "a-national" law, a *lex mercatoria,* is developing. This international law of commercial arbitration, the argument goes, combines some of the best, most well-worn and well-respected customs and practices of international commercial trade. It is, however, extremely difficult to identify the precise terms of this supposed a-national law, and it would be virtually unheard of for parties to choose *lex mercatoria* as the law governing their contracts. More appropriately, it may be said that the established customs and practices of international commercial trade are sometimes considered by arbitrators as a supplement to the specific national or state law chosen by the parties to govern their contractual relationship.

In both the international and the domestic arbitration contexts, however, judicial review is quite limited. Courts often suggest that "mere error" of fact or law by an arbitrator is not sufficient grounds for reversing an arbitral award. As a result, it is often suggested that arbitrators enjoy discretion to "do equity" even where the terms of a contract or governing law would otherwise compel another result. Statistics are not available on the extent to which arbitrators abandon the rule of law in favor of vague efforts to reach a "fair" result. The common view that arbitrators sometimes attempt to offer a partial victory to both sides or "split the baby," however, is often cited as a justification for avoiding arbitration.

Unconscionable
Arbitration Agreements

As we have seen, the fundamental basis for arbitration is the consent of the parties. There are many situations, however, where although there is a written contract with express terms providing for arbitration, signed by both parties, there may be some question as to whether one of the parties actually consented to the arbitration agreement. Typically, this issue arises in the context of standard-form agreements, offered by a large institution to an individual consumer (such as agreements to rent cars, provide telephone service, etc.). Although there is "consent" to the terms in a general sense, there is no bargaining. Such contracts are sometimes referred to as contracts of "adhesion." Under varying rules in various jurisdictions, such contracts may be subject to challenge. Where it can be shown that an arbitration provision in a contract is "unconscionable," the provision may be voided or modified.

A New York appellate court, for example, has held that arbitration filing fees charged by the International Chamber of Commerce were, in light of the value of the equipment at stake, so high as to make the arbitration clause in a standard form agreement unconscionable. See *Brower v. Gateway 2000, Inc.,* 676 N.Y.S.2d 569 (1st Dep't 1998). The Supreme Court of the United States, however, has held that claims that the possibility of high filing fees, or arbitrator fees, could impair a consumer's ability to vindicate statutory rights would not suffice to void an arbitration agreement. See *Green Tree Financial Corp. v. Randolph,* 531 U.S. 79 , 121 S.Ct. 513, 148 L.Ed.2d 373 (2000).

The outcome of a challenge to an arbitration clause on unconscionability grounds will generally depend on two factors. First, there is the question of the procedure by which the arbitration agreement was adopted. Although standard form, take-it-or-leave-it contracts are not *per se* unconscionable, where the form is confusing, or the arbitration clause is "buried," there may be some argument that consumers did not understand what they had signed. By contrast, although there is no strict requirement to do so, where the arbitration clause is highlighted, and where the consequences of arbitration are explained (no right to go to court, no jury trial, limited rights of appeal and review), there can be little argument that the objecting party was confused.

Second, there is the question of the substantive fairness of the arbitration clause. As noted above, such substantive challenges may take the form of an argument that the fees for arbitration are so high as to make it practically impossible for a consumer to vindicate his/her rights. Other substantive challenges have included claims that the arbitration process was fundamentally unfair in some way. For example, where the arbitrator is chosen exclusively by the institution, or where the individuals have only limited rights to present their claims or defenses, there may be an argument that the arbitration procedure is fundamentally unfair.

Where several potential procedural or substantive fairness problems appear in the same agreement, an arbitration clause may be particularly at risk. In *Powertel, Inc. v. Bexley*, 743 So.2d 570 (Fla. Dist. Ct. App. 1999), for example, the court held that an arbitration provision in a cellular telephone service agreement was unconscionable because (1) the arbitration provision was not in the original service agreement; (2) the amended arbitration provision was contained in a pamphlet, which arrived along with the customer's bill for service; (3) the amended arbitration clause was not conspicuous, and was indistinguishable from other advertisements and inserts consumers typically receive in their monthly bills; and (4) although consumers could reject the amendment, by cancelling service, such cancellation would result in loss of investment in purchased telephone equipment and loss of the user's assigned telephone number. These, and other problems, when piled one on top of the other, resulted in a finding of unconscionability.

The background, purpose, terms and practical implications of any arbitration agreement, together with the governing law of the applicable jurisdiction, will determine whether any claim of unconscionability will succeed. Moreover, the unconscionability doctrine cannot be applied in a disparate manner, to void an arbitration agreement where another type of agreement would pass muster. Nevertheless, under the FAA, states may regulate contracts generally, and may (on an equal basis) regulate arbitration agreements. Thus, where the procedure by which an arbitration clause is adopted is suspect, or where the terms of the clause are egregiously unfair, claims of unconscionability may succeed.

CONSTRUCTING AN ARBITRATION CLAUSE

There is no such thing as a standard form, one-size-fits-all arbitration clause. Just as parties choose to arbitrate for any number of reasons, so too they may choose a variety of different forms of arbitration to suit their purposes. In most instances, however, parties will not know in advance the precise shape of the disputes they will face in the future. For example, in a commercial agreement between supplier and customer, in deciding what is best for them in arbitration, the parties must predict who is likely to be plaintiff and defendant, how large the disputes are likely to be, and whether their resolution will require some special expertise or special form of proceeding.

Basic Issues

What follows is a check-list of some of the most basic issues that should be considered in constructing an arbitration clause. In each case, one or more of these issues may be of particular importance. There also may be other issues that assume special significance. Careful review of the circumstances of the parties, and their potential disputes, must be the ultimate guide to constructing an effective arbitration clause.

SHOULD THERE BE AN ARBITRATION CLAUSE?

It is possible to agree to arbitrate a dispute after it arises. "Submission agreements," by which parties agree to submit a specific dispute to arbitration in lieu of litigation, however, may be more difficult to agree on after-the-fact, when the dispute is raging. As a result, if the parties view arbitration as a desirable concept at the outset of their contractual relations, it is preferable to agree to the terms of arbitration in advance.

Under the FAA, and parallel state and international provisions, arbitration agreements must be in writing. Although there may be circumstances where agreement to arbitrate is inferred (e.g., where one contract document incorporates by reference another document containing an arbitration provision), the parties should not rely on oral promises, or some vague, unwritten understanding that they will arbitrate their disputes.

SHOULD THE PARTIES USE INSTITUTIONAL RULES AND ADMINISTRATION?

It is possible to conduct an arbitration without any involvement from an arbitration-sponsoring institution (such as the AAA, ICC or LCIA). These "ad hoc" arbitrations, in which the parties choose an arbitral tribunal by themselves, and conduct the arbitration without an independent administrator other than the arbitrator(s), can work and can be less costly than institutional arbitration. Further, it is possible to conduct an ad hoc arbitration, and borrow the rules of a sponsoring institution (to the extent applicable) for purposes of the arbitration without any intervention from the sponsoring institution.

Many parties, however, choose to conduct their arbitrations under the auspices of a sponsoring institution. A case administrator, independent of the arbitrator, can assist in handling the minutiae of the arbitration process (collecting arbitrator fees, scheduling conferences, distributing correspondence, etc.). The sponsoring institution, moreover, may be able to assist the parties in selecting a qualified arbitrator, and in ensuring that the arbitrator is unbiased. The use of a sponsoring institution, with well-established rules, can also lend stability to the arbitration process.

Where parties choose to arbitrate under the auspices of a specific sponsoring organization, their arbitration clause will typically state that the parties agree to arbitrate disputes before the named organization, using the named organization's rules. If the parties wish to make additions to, or exceptions from, those rules, they should expressly state their modifications in the arbitration clause. The rules of most sponsoring organizations generally state that the then-current rules of the organization apply unless the parties have otherwise agreed in their arbitration clause, or where the parties have otherwise agreed in the course of the arbitration process, once the process is initiated. If the parties wish to use the sponsoring institution's rules only, without subjecting themselves to administration by the institution, they should state as much expressly in their arbitration agreement.

Almost all of the major arbitration-sponsoring institutions have a form of arbitration clause that is recommended for use in establishing arbitration under their authority and rules. These forms are typically included with the current versions of the rules available from the sponsoring institutions.

SHOULD THE ARBITRATION CLAUSE BE BROAD OR NARROW?

Parties need not refer every potential dispute between them to arbitration. Indeed, parties often choose to send only certain matters (such as valuation of some property) to arbitration, reserving all other issues for conventional litigation. Because it is not always possible to anticipate all the disputes that may arise between the parties, so that they can be specifically enumerated in the arbitration clause, parties often choose "broad" arbitration clauses, which simply state that any claims or disputes between them that arise out of, or relate to, their contract, will be subject to arbitration.

Such broad arbitration clauses, however, may sweep more issues into arbitration than the parties might expect. Although the law is conflicting in different jurisdictions, the general rule is that a broad arbitration clause will be construed to reach issues beyond pure contract claims, so long as the claims relate to the contract. For example, in a commercial dispute, a party might claim that the other party's behavior breaches the contract, and also breaches some statute (such as the antitrust laws, or state unfair compensation law). A broad arbitration clause would most likely be held to require arbitration of all such claims.

If the parties go in the other direction and seek to construct a "narrow" clause, limited to only certain specific issues, there is a danger that, after a dispute arises, the parties will waste time wrangling over whether all or only part of the dispute is subject to arbitration. Clever counsel often seek to characterize claims in such a way as to avoid a narrow arbitration clause.

There is no good solution to this dilemma, other than to be aware of the conflicting concerns. Where parties intend to construct a broad arbitration provision, they should use expansive terms, such as "all disputes arising out of or relating to" the contract. If they mean to construct a narrow provision, they should be precise in the choice of issues referable to arbitration.

WHO DECIDES WHAT THE ARBITRATION CLAUSE MEANS?

The involvement of courts in regulating an arbitration can affect the speed and cost of the process. When an arbitration is initiated, and one of the parties contends that the claims submitted for arbitration are not covered by the arbitration clause, there is a risk that court proceedings will be initiated to challenge the arbitration, thus interrupting the process. The best solution is to state that matters concerning the meaning of the arbitration clause, including the jurisdiction of the arbitrator to resolve issues in the case, is to be resolved by the arbitrator, at least in the first instance. Ultimately, after the arbitrator issues an award, there may be recourse to a court to challenge the award, but subsequent review by a court is much less disruptive of the process.

In the absence of an express statement that the arbitrator has juris-diction to decide his or her own jurisdiction, there is a serious risk that, when jurisdictional issues arise, they will lead to litigation that can interrupt the arbitration process. Indeed, the Supreme Court has held that courts are presumptively authorized to rule on arbitration jurisdiction issues, unless the parties have otherwise agreed. See *First Options of Chicago, Inc. v. Kaplan,* 514 U.S. 938, 115 S.Ct. 1920, 131 L.Ed.2d 985 (1995).

HOW SHOULD THE ARBITRATOR BE CHOSEN?

The choice of an arbitrator may be critical to the outcome of arbi-tration proceedings. Parties can simply identify a specific arbitra-tor in their arbitration clause, but there is always the possibility that the named arbitrator will be unable or unwilling to serve. Parties can also leave the matter of selection of an arbitrator entirely to a third party, such as an arbitration-sponsoring institu-tion. The ability to choose an arbitrator who is "right" for the dis-pute, however, is often one of the most attractive elements of arbi-tration. As a result, parties often frame a mechanism by which they can jointly participate in the arbitrator-selection process. One method is for each party to choose its own arbitrator. These two party-chosen arbitrators thereafter confer, and choose a third "independent" arbitrator. This method can be expensive and time-consuming.

Another method allows the sponsoring institution to produce a list of names of qualified potential arbitrators, which the parties can review, and strike one or more whom they do not prefer (much like peremptory challenges in jury selection). From the remaining candidates, the arbitrator(s) will be selected.

Still another method is to name a particular institution, rather than a specific person, as the arbitrator for disputes. For example, the parties might agree that any accounting issues between them will be resolved by arbitration before an independent accounting firm, with the specific arbitrator to be chosen by the accounting firm.

Whatever selection method is chosen, the key issues are generally whether the arbitrator(s) will have specific expertise in the applicable area, and the degree to which the parties will control the selection of the arbitrator(s). Most sponsoring organizations also have rules on the independence of arbitrators, providing the parties with disclosure of facts that may establish bias or conflicts concerning potential arbitrators, and allowing the parties to challenge selection of particular arbitrators on such grounds.

Ultimately, if the method of arbitrator selection specified in an arbitration clause fails, the FAA and parallel state statutes permit courts to intervene and select an arbitrator to preserve the effectiveness of an arbitration agreement.

WHAT LAW DO THE PARTIES CHOOSE AND WHAT PLACE OF ARBITRATION?

One of the first issues, and often a critical question, once an arbitration proceeding begins, concerns the substantive law to be applied by the arbitration tribunal. If the parties have not specified the law that will govern interpretation and enforcement of their contract, the arbitrators may spend considerable time and effort resolving conflict-of-law issues. Often, choice of law will turn on a factual inquiry as to where the contract was negotiated, signed and performed. Because such factors can point in different directions, an express choice of law in a contract can dramatically expedite the arbitration process.

Similarly, an express choice of location for arbitration proceedings can have a significant effect on the procedural course of the arbitration. Generally, when issues arise as to the conduct of an arbitration, the courts in the location where the arbitration is taking place will have jurisdiction to resolve any disputes (e.g., problems in selecting an arbitrator, or issuance of a subpoena to gather evidence for use in the arbitration). The choice of location for the arbitration thus constitutes an implicit choice of the courts at that location for resolution of arbitration procedure disputes, and the courts at that location will generally apply the procedural rules applicable in that jurisdiction.

Choice of location for the arbitration may have other practical consequences. Many sponsoring organizations make a special effort to select an arbitrator with some connection to the arbitral forum. Further, the choice of forum can affect the cost of the proceedings, depending on such things as expenses for travel and accommodations for the parties, witnesses and their counsel.

How Is the Award to Be Enforced?

The arbitration process generally results in an award, which may grant relief, or which may determine that a party asserting a claim has no right to relief. The award may be quite simple (only a few lines) or may be supported by detailed findings of fact and conclusions of law. The parties may specify in their arbitration clause what form of award they prefer.

The parties may also specify the form of judicial review that is available once the award is announced. Parties may provide that an arbitration award is entirely non-binding. In that event, if the parties do not voluntarily comply with the award, or otherwise settle their dispute, litigation may proceed as if no arbitration proceedings had occurred.

More often, however, parties provide that any arbitration award will be final and binding. Despite such language, parties generally preserve their rights under the FAA and parallel state statutes to have limited review of an arbitration award for egregious problems, such as the corruption of an arbitrator. Mere errors of fact or law, however, are not generally sufficient to upset an arbitration. Some courts have suggested, however, that parties may provide for heightened standards of judicial review by so specifying in an arbitration clause.

An arbitration clause will also often provide that a petition to review or enforce an arbitration clause may be made in one or more specified courts. Generally, under the FAA, such review may be had in a court at the location where the arbitration took place. The Supreme Court has made clear, however, that such jurisdiction is not exclusive, and the parties may otherwise provide for review by a court in another location. See *Cortez Byrd Chips, Inc. v. Bill Harbert Construction Co.*, 529 U.S. 193, 120 S.Ct. 1331, 146 L. Ed. 2d 171 (2000).

Additional Considerations

In addition to the most basic issues outlined above, parties may wish to consider a host of other provisions that may be added to an arbitration clause. In many instances, if the parties do not make express choices on these subjects and simply adopt the rules of an arbitration-sponsoring institution, the institutional rules will "fill in the gaps" with solutions that may be satisfactory to the parties. If the parties have a clear preference on these issues, however, they should write those preferences into the arbitration clause whenever possible.

MIGHT THERE BE A NEED FOR PRELIMINARY RELIEF?

Ordinarily, an arbitration decision is not effective until there is a "final" award. The award, once entered, can be taken to a court for entry as a judgment, which may be enforced through normal court procedures. There may, however, be circumstances where preliminary relief is required before a final award can be entered. Such relief, for example, is often appropriate in intellectual property disputes. The parties may provide that the arbitration tribunal is empowered to issue interim awards, which can be enforced in the same manner as final awards. Alternatively, the parties may provide that preliminary relief may be sought directly from a court, while the arbitration is pending. The arbitration law in many jurisdictions permits such applications, to preserve the *status quo*. An express contractual provision permitting such applications, however, avoids the possibility that a party may be considered to have waived its arbitration rights by making an application to a court concerning a dispute that is otherwise subject to arbitration.

IS THERE A NEED FOR SPECIFIC PROCEDURAL RULES?

Typically, arbitrators enjoy wide discretion in the conduct of arbitration proceedings. Institutional rules and governing statutes generally require little more than fundamental due process (notice and an opportunity to be heard). Discovery is often limited, and evidentiary and procedural rules during a hearing are usually quite relaxed. Indeed, the very reason that parties choose arbitration may be that informal procedures can save time and expense.

The parties may, however, choose one or more elements of formal court procedures for their particular needs. It may be important, for example, to have the opportunity to take deposition discovery (not usually used in arbitration). If the parties so agree, then that discovery process will be available.

Similarly, the parties may wish to adopt specific procedures for the hearing of their disputes. For example, although most arbitrators will permit thorough cross-examination and a right to present expert testimony, the parties may wish to establish specific procedures reinforcing the existence of these rights.

More formal procedures should be adopted with great care. In addition to impairing the speed and efficiency of arbitration, the establishment of detailed procedures may jeopardize the award granted by the arbitrator. Generally, awards are subject to very limited review by the courts. The more specific the procedures, the more likely it is that an award can be upset as a result of mistakes in the application of the procedures.

WILL THERE BE A NEED FOR CONSOLIDATED PROCEEDINGS?

Because arbitration is a creature of contract, parties cannot be compelled to arbitrate without an express agreement to arbitrate. This problem arises in multi-party disputes where some, but not all, of the parties have agreed to arbitrate. The addition of another party as an additional claimant, additional respondent, or third-party respondent, is impossible without the consent of all other parties. As a matter of efficiency, the parties to an arbitration contract may agree, in advance, that other parties may be added to the arbitration, without further agreement, so long as the additional parties also agree to participate in the arbitration.

Such a clause would make it easier, for example, to deal with a dispute between manufacturer and buyer, where sales agents and other intermediaries may also have been involved. In the absence of such a clause, duplicative arbitration and parallel litigation might be required.

WHAT DEGREE OF CONFIDENTIALITY IS REQUIRED FOR THE PROCEEDING?

Generally, arbitration law and custom recognize that arbitration proceedings are private. The rules of most arbitration-sponsoring organizations, moreover, provide that arbitration proceedings and awards are confidential, unless the parties otherwise agree.

The parties may choose more or less restrictive confidentiality proceedings for various reasons. In intellectual property disputes, for
example, it may be extremely important to maintain the security of
a secret process or invention. The parties may wish to grant the
arbitrator the power to enter a confidentiality order, or may even
provide, in advance, the terms of such an order. Typically, such
orders provide that all documents and other evidence exchanged
between the parties will be kept confidential, and returned or
destroyed after the proceedings are concluded. The parties may
also wish to specify the procedure for dealing with subpoenas from
non-parties to the arbitration or other requests for information that
seek documents, pleadings or testimony from the arbitration.

Do the Parties Wish to Place Time Limits on the Proceedings?

Although one hallmark of arbitration has been its speed, as
opposed to time-consuming proceedings in court, such is not
always the case. Moreover, in some instances, the parties may
have a particular interest in obtaining a speedy resolution of their
disputes. For these reasons, parties sometimes place time limits on
the arbitration process.

Such time limits may be applied at all stages of the proceedings.
The parties may require, for example, that the arbitrator(s) be
selected within a fixed period. If the selections are not made on
time, the parties may provide for an alternate method of selection
(such as having a neutral party, or an arbitration-sponsoring institution, complete the arbitrator selection process).

Similarly, the parties may require that any hearing of a dispute be
completed within a stated period, or that the arbitrator's award be
issued within a specific time after the close of the hearing. Such
limitations may mean that the form of the arbitration process will
be affected. To complete the arbitration on time, the arbitrator
might need to limit the number of witnesses or the length of their

testimony, for example. To issue an award quickly, the arbitrator might create an award that resolves the dispute without any statement of reasons or factual findings.

WHAT REMEDIAL POWERS SHOULD THE ARBITRATOR HAVE?

Although arbitrators generally enjoy broad powers to resolve disputes, there are occasions when an arbitrator's authority may be unclear, in the absence of express agreement of the parties. For this reason, parties may wish to specify, in their arbitration agreement, precisely what the arbitrator can and cannot do.

Parties may specify, for example, that an arbitrator may grant equitable remedies, including specific performance of the contract at issue. Similarly, they may provide that the arbitrator can award pre-judgment interest, and may specify the rate and method of calculating interest. Further, they may state whether the arbitrator is authorized to award punitive damages, and may even state the conditions under which such damages would be appropriate.

The parties may also provide for remedies that grow out of the arbitration process itself. It is common, for example, to state that the arbitrator may impose attorneys' fees and costs on the losing party. The parties may also wish to define what "costs" can be included in such an award. The parties may, alternatively, provide that attorneys' fees will be borne individually by each party, and that the costs of arbitration will be borne equally, no matter the result of the arbitration.

DOES THE INTERNATIONAL CHARACTER OF THE DISPUTE REQUIRE SPECIAL PROVISIONS?

Whole volumes have been written on the unique subject of arbitration of international disputes (i.e., disputes between citizens of two different countries, or where the property or transaction at issue may involve more than one country's legal system). A more complete discussion of the international aspects of arbitration appears later in this book.

Here, it is sufficient to state that special provisions are often used for arbitration of international disputes. It is common, for example, to provide that any neutral arbitrator in an international dispute will be a citizen of a nation other than the home countries of the disputants.

Special attention must also be paid to the location for the arbitration proceedings. Because the law of the country where the arbitration takes place will generally govern the procedure for the arbitration, it is important to consider whether the local arbitration law serves the needs of the disputants.

The international character of the dispute, moreover, may require consideration of some practical aspects of the conduct of the arbitration. It may be necessary, for example, to specify what language will be spoken during the arbitration. Provision for interpreter services may also be required. Choice of an arbitration location may also have practical consequences. Selection of a location, for example, may affect the cost of transportation, lodging and communication.

Even the question of what currency denomination will be used in the award may be addressed in the arbitration clause. Absent an express agreement, in advance, on such practical issues, either the parties will have to resolve such questions in the heat of the arbitration battle, when agreement is less likely to occur, or the matter will have to be resolved by the arbitrator, taking up time and resources that could be better spent resolving the principal dispute.

WHAT LEVEL OF JUDICIAL REVIEW IS DESIRED?

It is common for arbitration provisions to state that any award in arbitration will be "final and binding" on the parties. Despite such language, the provisions of the FAA and parallel state statutes will generally permit at least limited review of the award. Typically, however, such review is highly deferential, based on a presumption in favor of enforcing the award. Courts frequently state, for example, that "mere" errors of fact or law will not suffice to upset an award.

If the parties desire it, more searching judicial review of the award may be authorized in the arbitration agreement. Establishment of a stringent standard, however, may not alone suffice to permit detailed review of the correctness of the award. Many arbitration proceedings are conducted without any stenographic record, and it is not unusual for an arbitrator to issue an award without any statement of the reasons for the decision. Provision for a record of the proceedings and a more detailed statement of reasons for the award may assist the process of judicial review of any award.

CONDUCTING AN
ARBITRATION

This chapter deals with the conduct of an arbitration, from commencement through the point at which an award is rendered. The conduct of any particular arbitration proceeding will vary, depending on the agreement of the parties, the institutional rules (if any) chosen, and the preferences of the arbitrator(s). This chapter outlines procedures and issues that are common to most arbitration proceedings.

Preserving the Right to Arbitrate

AGREEMENT, MODIFICATION AND WAIVER

Arbitration generally proceeds only by consent of the parties. The FAA, and comparable state statutes, generally require that an agreement to arbitrate a dispute be in writing. Although it is possible to agree to arbitrate after a dispute arises, it is often difficult to agree on dispute resolution procedures in such circumstances. Thus, if arbitration is the preferred method of dispute resolution, it is important to specify the choice of arbitration, in writing, in advance of any dispute.

Even after a dispute arises, however, it is always possible for parties to modify their arbitration agreement. Such modifications may be reflected as formal contract amendments. More often, parties stipulate to specific procedures for arbitration of a dispute, even though the original arbitration agreement said nothing about the particular procedures (or even included language to the contrary).The rules of many arbitration-sponsoring organizations expressly permit such modifications.

Once a dispute arises, a party must take reasonable steps to invoke the arbitration agreement, or risk a claim of waiver of the right to arbitrate. Where there is a valid arbitration agreement covering an existing dispute, and a party nevertheless commences a lawsuit regarding the dispute, it may be concluded that the party does not wish to rely on its right to arbitrate. If the other party to the dispute similarly agrees to pursue litigation in court (evidenced, for example, by answering the complaint without invoking the arbitration agreement), the parties may continue to litigate. Again, arbitration is a matter of agreement, and parties may modify their original agreement by choosing not to arbitrate a particular dispute.

Because of the risk of a claim of waiver of the right to arbitrate, it is important for a party to take steps to invoke an arbitration agreement whenever arbitration is the preferred method of dispute resolution. In some circumstances, participation in a lawsuit may not be considered waiver of an arbitration right. For example, requests for preliminary relief from a court that are related to an arbitration proceeding may not constitute a waiver of arbitration rights. In general, however, any active participation in litigation, without invocation of an arbitration agreement, risks a claim of waiver of the right to arbitrate.

JUDICIAL ENFORCEMENT OF AGREEMENTS TO ARBITRATE

Arbitration agreements, to a large extent, are embraced and implemented by parties without any need for judicial intervention.

When a party refuses to honor an arbitration agreement, however, a party wishing to preserve the right to arbitrate generally may proceed in one of two ways.

First, a party may initiate an arbitration proceeding and provide appropriate notice to the adverse party. If the respondent chooses not to appear and respond to the claims, an award may be obtained by default. The rules of the sponsoring organization, or the arbitrator, may require that the claimant make some showing in support of the default award. Once the default award is rendered, it may be enforced like any other arbitration award. The respondent may claim, in opposing enforcement of the default award, that the award was improper for some fundamental reason (such as that the arbitration agreement did not extend to the claims on which the default award was rendered). The defaulting respondent, however, generally will not be able to argue about the merits of the award.

The second alternative for the party seeking to enforce an arbitration provision is to move to compel arbitration. Such a motion may arise as a response to a lawsuit. Thus, for example, if a valid arbitration agreement exists, and one party nevertheless initiates a lawsuit, the opposing party may move to stay the litigation and to compel arbitration of the dispute. As noted previously, failure to make such a motion to compel arbitration may be construed as waiver of the right to arbitrate.

Even where there is no litigation, if one party refuses to participate in arbitration of a dispute, the other party may initiate a proceeding in court to compel arbitration. In that event, the opposing party must generally identify any reasons why the arbitration is improper. If the court issues an order compelling arbitration, and the opposing party nevertheless refuses to participate in the arbitration proceeding, the default award may not be subject to any of the challenges that the opposing party raised (or could have raised) in opposing the motion to compel arbitration.

The party opposing arbitration may take steps to restrain the arbitration process. The party opposing arbitration may attempt to convince the arbitrator that some part of the arbitration proceeding is improper. For example, the party might claim that the arbitration agreement does not cover some aspects of the dispute. In some jurisdictions, moreover, a party opposing arbitration may commence an independent proceeding in court, for declaratory or injunctive relief, to halt or modify some aspect of the arbitration proceeding that party believes to be improper.

Commencing an Arbitration

INVOKING THE ARBITRATION AGREEMENT

A party seeking to invoke an arbitration agreement generally must provide some notice to the opposing party of the nature of the dispute, the contractual basis for arbitration of the dispute and any other matters that the parties' agreement (or the applicable rules of any sponsoring organization) may require, such as the amount or type of relief requested. Generally, such notice is called a "demand" for arbitration.

A demand for arbitration need not be as detailed as a complaint in litigation. Often an arbitration-sponsoring organization will provide a short form of demand, which can be quickly and easily executed. Depending on the rules and the agreement of the parties, no formal pleadings may be required for the arbitration.

It is common, however, at least in commercial arbitration, to provide a statement of claim (much like a complaint), which accompanies the demand for arbitration. In some instances, moreover, where the claimant has not clearly articulated its claim, either in the demand for arbitration or in a statement of claim, the arbitrator may request that the claimant specify the claim in a pleading or pre-hearing brief of some kind.

Because arbitration is generally a matter of contract, it is also common for the rules of sponsoring organizations to require that the party initiating an arbitration specify the arbitration clause, or other agreement, which serves as the basis for the arbitration proceeding. Often, the claimant is required to attach a copy of the clause or agreement to its initial papers. In this way, the opposing party, the sponsoring organization and the arbitrator can immediately determine the basis for, and the scope of, the arbitration.

Agreements and rules vary, but generally there is some requirement that the initiating papers (demand for arbitration, statement of claim or other documents) be served on the respondent. The method of service may be specified in the parties' agreement or in the rules the parties have chosen to govern arbitration of disputes. Where no method of service has been specified, it is generally preferable to err on the side of providing more notice rather than less. Thus, service may be made by personal delivery (with confirmation of receipt), by registered mail (return receipt) or by multiple alternative methods (mail, overnight delivery, telefax, etc.). Ultimately, the initiating party's goal is to be able to establish, for the arbitrator or any court reviewing the matter, that the respondent was properly notified of the commencement of the arbitration.

Where a sponsoring organization is involved, copies of the initiating papers generally must be filed with the sponsoring organization, and a filing fee paid. Often, the size of the filing fee is keyed to the size of the claim. The sponsoring organization may also require that the claimant provide proof of service of initiating papers on the respondent. Some sponsoring organizations also provide a mechanism by which the organization will notify the respondent of the commencement of the arbitration, and the organization may serve the respondent with copies of the initiating papers.

Where the parties have not chosen an arbitration-sponsoring organization, the initiating papers generally need not be filed anywhere. Once an arbitrator is chosen, however, copies of the initiating papers generally must be provided to the arbitrator.

ANSWERING THE DEMAND

The rules of most arbitration-sponsoring organizations give respondents the option to serve and file papers in response to the demand for arbitration and statement of claim (if any). Like the initiating papers, any answering papers may be quite brief and informal. Often, parties will simply exchange letters outlining claims and any defenses to the claims.

In many instances, for strategic reasons, the respondent may choose not to serve an answering statement. (The respondent may not have enough facts to prepare such a statement, or the respondent may wish to avoid limiting its positions in the arbitration.) If the respondent chooses not to serve an answering statement, the rules of most organizations provide that the claims are generally denied. The respondent often has the opportunity at a later point (for example, in pre-hearing briefs) to articulate its position.

Where the parties have not chosen an arbitration-sponsoring organization or its rules, the requirement to serve an answering statement will depend upon the agreement of the parties and the directions of the arbitrator. In the case of an *ad hoc* arbitration, it may be desirable to seek guidance from the arbitrator on any deadline for filing an answering statement, and the consequences (if any) of failure to respond to the claimant's arbitration-initiating papers.

COUNTERCLAIMS

The rules of most sponsoring organizations permit the respondent in an arbitration to serve, in addition to any answering statement in response to the initial claims, a statement of any counterclaims by the respondent against the claimant. Like the claimant's initiating papers, the statement of any counterclaims may be informal or more like a formal pleading in court. The rules of the various sponsoring organizations, moreover, provide different periods during which counterclaims must be stated. Often, after such period has elapsed, permission from the arbitrator or sponsoring organization must be obtained before serving a counterclaim.

The consequences of failure to serve a counterclaim vary, depending on the rules of the sponsoring organization and the law in the applicable jurisdiction. In general, however, where the potential counterclaim is related to the initial claim, there is a risk that failure to assert the counterclaim will be deemed *res judicata* on the matters that could have been asserted in the counterclaim. That is, the respondent who is given an opportunity to assert a counterclaim, but who forgoes that opportunity, may be deemed to have waived the right to assert the counterclaim. This rule in arbitration parallels similar rules regarding compulsory counterclaims in ordinary civil litigation.

When a counterclaim is pursued, the rules of most sponsoring organizations require filing of the counterclaim and service on the adversary, in a manner comparable to that required by the rules for initiating a claim. Although a respondent (under some rules) may not be required to pay any administrative fee for participation in an arbitration, often a fee will be required for the filing of a counterclaim. Generally, the amount of the fee will depend on the size of the counterclaim.

CONSOLIDATION

Because arbitration is generally the product of an agreement between parties, a party cannot be compelled to participate in an arbitration proceeding without its consent. Similarly, even where arbitration agreements exist, one party to an arbitration agreement generally cannot be compelled to consolidate its claims or defenses with those of another party, without mutual consent.

Thus, for example, the owner of a property might have an agreement with a lender that includes a provision for arbitration. The owner might have a separate contract with a general contractor for a construction project on the property that also provides for arbitration of disputes. In the event of a problem on the project, the owner might prefer to have a single arbitration proceeding, in which all the claims and defenses of the owner against the lender and the contractor could be resolved. Because the lender and the contractor never agreed to participate in an arbitration with each other, however, they could not be compelled to consolidate the hearing of their claims and defenses without their mutual consent.

The requirement for mutual consent to arbitration generally applies even when consolidation might avoid duplicative litigation. For example, where parties have agreed to arbitrate some, but not all of their disputes, at least two proceedings (the arbitration and any other litigation on the inarbitrable issues) must be pursued to provide a complete resolution of the issues. The understandable desire to avoid such duplication, however, generally will not suffice to compel consolidation of the claims.

For similar reasons, it is virtually impossible to pursue a class action through arbitration. The rules of the major sponsoring organizations do not contemplate such a procedural device, and there is little possibility of obtaining mutual consent to such a procedure from all affected parties.

Despite these general limitations, it may be possible to obtain consolidation in some cases. If consolidation is considered important, a procedure for consolidation should be written into the original arbitration agreements. If the importance of consolidation becomes apparent only after a dispute arises, a party's success in obtaining consolidation may depend on negotiation and persuasive pressure from an arbitrator or case administrator at an arbitration-sponsoring organization.

SELECTION OF ARBITRATORS

Selection of arbitrators, like most other procedures in arbitration, is largely a matter of consent. In some instances, parties may agree in advance of any dispute to arbitrate their claims before a specific person or entity (such as an accounting firm, which may choose the specific arbitrator when the dispute arises). Specification of the arbitrator in advance can save time and permit greater vetting of the arbitrator's skills and experience. After a dispute arises, however, parties may have second thoughts about their chosen arbitrator, and in some instances the chosen arbitrator will not be available to serve. Parties may also agree on the choice of an arbitrator after a dispute arises (and may then modify any prior agreement on choice of an arbitrator).

In instances in which the parties have not agreed on an arbitrator, the arbitration-sponsoring organization that the parties have chosen will assist them in selecting an arbitrator. Under one common method, the organization will put together a list of potential arbitrators. The parties have the opportunity to strike some number of the candidates, and to list the remainder in order of preference. The highest-ranked of the mutually acceptable candidates is then chosen as arbitrator.

Another common selection method (especially in international arbitration) is for each party to choose one arbitrator, and for these two arbitrators to choose the third arbitrator. The third arbitrator must be neutral, and generally serves as chair of the panel.

Many arbitration-sponsoring organizations, as part of their service, conduct screening of potential arbitrators. Qualifications may include prior experience and training in arbitration, expertise in particular subjects, geographical proximity to the parties and availability to serve. Many organizations also train potential arbitrators, and provide a system for obtaining feedback on the performance of arbitrators, once chosen. As a result, parties often choose sponsoring organizations in part based on their expected ability to provide assistance in selecting a qualified, appropriate arbitrator in the event of a dispute.

When one or more of the parties fail to exercise choices in selecting arbitrators, the rules of most arbitration-sponsoring organizations provide various methods by which the organization will select an arbitrator for the parties. If all else fails, moreover, the FAA and parallel state statutes permit an application to a court for assistance in appointment of an arbitrator.

GROUNDS FOR DISQUALIFICATION OF ARBITRATORS

The rules of most arbitration-sponsoring organizations require that neutral arbitrators (as opposed to party-appointed arbitrators) avoid the appearance of impropriety or bias in their service as arbitrators. The FAA and parallel state statutes, moreover, may permit a challenge to an award made by an arbitrator with an undisclosed, material bias or interest affecting the case. As a result, the rules of most sponsoring organizations provide for a system of disclosure of potential bias or interest in the case, and challenge of an arbitrator candidate on such basis. Generally, any challenge is resolved by an administrator at the organization, rather than by the arbitrator candidate. Failure to lodge a challenge when facts concerning a potential bias or interest are disclosed generally will constitute waiver of the right to challenge an award on the basis of an alleged bias or interest of an arbitrator.

The rules of most sponsoring organizations, moreover, provide that, if during the course of proceedings any bias or interest becomes apparent, an arbitrator must disclose the issue; a challenge system similar to the process used at the outset of the proceedings generally applies. Because of the inefficiency involved in replacing an arbitrator after a proceeding is under way, it is preferable to explore issues of bias or interest at the outset of the case. For this reason, parties are generally encouraged to disclose the identities of lawyers, witnesses and affiliated parties at the outset of the proceedings to make it easier for arbitrators to determine whether they must disclose some prior connection to the dispute or to the parties.

PREHEARING DISCOVERY

Prehearing discovery procedures may vary greatly, depending on the agreement of the parties, the sponsoring organization and its rules, the predilections of the arbitrator(s) and the circumstances of the case. In general, however, parties often choose arbitration in part because it can avoid some of the cost and burden of discovery devices available in ordinary civil litigation. Therefore, certain discovery devices, such as interrogatories, bills of particulars, or requests for admission, are almost unthinkable in arbitration. Others, like depositions, are possible but still rare.

What has become the norm in arbitration, at least in commercial arbitration in the United States, is the exchange of documents pertinent to a dispute. Essential documents, such as any contract or correspondence between the parties, as well as such items as invoices and payment records pertaining to the transaction, may be exchanged as a matter of course. More burdensome, time-consuming demands (wholesale fishing expeditions through rooms full of documents) are rarer. Generally, an arbitrator will weigh cost and delay factors involved in broad discovery more carefully than most judges and magistrates do in ordinary civil litigation.

The arbitration process, moreover, often permits swift identification of key issues and documents pertinent to a dispute. Many arbitrators conduct preliminary conferences at which the parties are encouraged to outline their positions, to agree upon matters that are not in controversy and to establish a protocol for exchange of any documents that may be critical to disputed points.

Often, moreover, an arbitrator will require pre-hearing briefs from the parties. This process may make it easier for parties to prepare for any hearing, and to identify any documents or witnesses that they may require to present their arguments and to respond to arguments from the other side.

Generally, when a party can identify specific documents or witnesses that are essential to a fair and rational disposition of a case, an arbitrator will expect that such documents or witnesses be produced. Failure to produce in circumstances in which the need is obvious may lead the arbitrator to make an adverse inference (that the missing document or witness would have been adverse) against the party that fails to produce the missing information.

PROVISIONAL REMEDIES

Absent specific authority in an arbitration agreement or rules agreed upon by the parties, it is unclear whether an arbitrator can, or will, issue an order granting provisional remedies. Such remedies (preliminary injunction, attachment of assets and the like), however, may be essential to preserve the *status quo* pending the resolution of the dispute through arbitration. Accordingly, when a party contemplates that there may be a need for such relief, it is desirable to write specific authorization for provisional remedies into an arbitration agreement, or to choose rules of a sponsoring organization that will permit the arbitrator to grant such remedies.

Generally, an order for provisional remedies from an arbitrator will take the form of an interim award, ordering the parties to take certain steps pending conclusion of the arbitration proceedings. The arbitration agreement or rules of the arbitration-sponsoring organization should provide that such an interim award may be enforced by court order, in the same manner as a final award of the arbitrator. Absent specific agreement or rules, there might be some question whether a non-final award could be enforced.

Even absent authority in an agreement or rules of a sponsoring organization, arbitration law in many jurisdictions permits an application to a court for provisional relief in aid of arbitration.

Such an application is generally considered to be ancillary to the arbitration, rather than a substitute for it. Thus, application to a court for provisional relief in aid of arbitration generally would not be considered a waiver of the right to arbitrate.

SETTING A HEARING DATE

Some arbitration agreements, and rules of some sponsoring organizations, set time limits for completion of a hearing. An agreement might provide, for example, that any hearing must be completed within three months of the date of appointment of the arbitrator, and that an award must be rendered within two weeks after completion of the hearing. If such restrictive time limits apply to an arbitration, it will be important for the parties to select an arbitrator who is available to conduct a hearing promptly.

More generally, however, most arbitration agreements say nothing on the question of the schedule for a hearing, or expressly leave the matter to the arbitrator's discretion. Often, as a result, an important part of the arbitrator's inquiry in any preliminary conference on a case will be to ask each party how long it will require to present its case, and to determine what dates are mutually convenient for the arbitrator, counsel, the parties and witnesses.

Because most arbitrators are busy, accomplished professionals, it is often difficult to conduct hearings over extended, unbroken periods of time. It is not unusual, as a result, for arbitrators to put a premium on compressing the number of in-person evidentiary hearings. In some instances, an arbitrator may set a time limit for the presentation of each side's case. In other instances, the arbitrator may set aside one or more days for the principal hearing of the case, and suggest that the parties must make some showing of need for any additional hearing time. Very often, moreover, an arbitrator will conduct hearings as his or her schedule permits. Unlike a jury trial, for example, arbitration hearings need not be conducted on consecutive days.

An arbitrator must bear in mind, however, that the FAA and parallel state statutes require that each party be given an opportunity to present its case. Fundamental due process concepts of notice and an opportunity to be heard, familiar to most lawyers and arbitrators, are generally implemented in arbitration proceedings.

Hearing Procedures

THE ROLE OF THE ARBITRATOR

Except where the parties have specifically agreed, or applicable rules of a sponsoring organization govern on a specific point, the arbitrator decides all matters of procedure and evidence during a hearing. Where three arbitrators sit as a panel, one arbitrator generally will serve as chairperson, who may call hearings to order and handle some administrative details. Decisions on procedure and evidence, however, will be made by majority vote of all the arbitrators.

Most arbitrators emphasize the desirability of agreement between the parties on as much of the procedural and evidentiary framework of the proceeding as possible. It is common, for example, for parties to stipulate to basic background facts and to the authenticity of most documents. Arbitrators also often encourage parties to narrow and sharpen the issues in a case, to permit more efficient hearing of proof and rendering of a focused award.

Although the atmosphere of most arbitration hearings, at least in the United States, remains adversarial, there is also an inquisitorial element. That is, arbitrators (who are often experienced lawyers, former judges or professionals in other areas) may take a very active role in reviewing the facts of a case. It is not unusual for arbitrators to ask questions of witnesses and counsel. It is also not unusual for arbitrators to call for the production of documents or other evidence that may be necessary to resolution of the dispute. In appropriate cases, an arbitrator may ask for a site visit, or inspection of machinery, even if the parties have not suggested it.

Most arbitrators see themselves as charged with a duty to do what is fair and efficient in order to gather facts needed to resolve a dispute. Although the views of the parties will be important indicators of how to proceed, an arbitrator may exercise considerable discretion in choosing appropriate procedures for a particular case.

SUBPOENAS

The FAA and parallel state statutes permit arbitrators to issue subpoenas for the attendance of non-party witnesses at an arbitration hearing. More often, such subpoenas are requested by one of the parties, rather than issued by arbitrators on their own initiative. Witness fees and travel expenses for witnesses subject to subpoena in arbitration are generally the same as those for witnesses subject to subpoena in court. Such subpoenas may be enforced by court order, as with an ordinary subpoena.

In most instances, witnesses comply voluntarily with subpoenas. Because of the burden on a party that can arise from the need to seek court assistance to enforce a subpoena for the testimony of a reluctant witness, however, arbitrators will often permit secondary evidence to fill in the gaps that a missing witness might otherwise fill. In general, evidentiary rules as to hearsay are much more flexible in arbitration than in ordinary civil litigation.

REPRESENTATION BY COUNSEL

Many state statutes, and the rules of most arbitration-sponsoring organizations, expressly preserve the right to representation by counsel in arbitration. In some rare instances, parties may seek to establish the informality of arbitration proceedings by specifying that such proceedings will involve the parties only, without lawyers. Most arbitration proceedings, however, are conducted with the assistance of lawyers.

Generally, lawyers for the parties identify themselves by serving and filing (with the sponsoring organization, where necessary) initial papers regarding the dispute. Ethical rules in individual states and countries vary. In general, however, representing a party to an arbitration does not require admission to practice, or *pro hac vice* temporary admission, in the jurisdiction where arbitration hearings may occur. Representation at any court proceedings ancillary to the arbitration (such as enforcement of an award) will, however, require admission to practice.

EX PARTE HEARINGS

Consistent with the basic due process concepts of notice and an opportunity to be heard, the rules of most arbitration-sponsoring organizations specify that it is impermissible to submit facts and argument to an arbitrator on an *ex parte* basis. Hearings are conducted in open sessions, and briefs and correspondence are sent to arbitrators with copies to adversaries or their counsel. Without specific authority from the parties, moreover, arbitrators are not authorized to conduct *ex parte* settlement discussions or to attempt to mediate the dispute through "shuttle diplomacy."

The rules of most sponsoring organizations, however, do not require that parties attend every arbitration hearing. So long as adequate notice of a hearing is given to all parties, an arbitrator may conduct a hearing even though one party chooses not to attend.

Indeed, it is possible in an arbitration proceeding to obtain a form of default judgment. Where a party has been notified of the commencement of an arbitration proceeding and chooses not to respond, the initiating party may pursue the appointment of an arbitrator, and the rendering of an award, without input from the adverse party. In most instances, such an award will not be rendered without some minimal showing of a basis for the award. In effect, an arbitrator will conduct a short, *ex parte* hearing, at which the initiating party must show, at least in outline form, what proof supports the rendering of the award.

An *ex parte* award is subject to challenge on a number of grounds, such as the lack of jurisdiction of the arbitrator and inadequacy of notice. As a result, in lieu of seeking a default award, a party may prefer to petition a court for an order compelling the adverse party to participate in the proceeding. If, despite such an order, the party nevertheless refuses to respond, any *ex parte* award may be subject to fewer challenges when the post-award judicial enforcement proceedings are commenced.

ORDER OF PROCEEDINGS

Individual agreements and rules aside, the order of most arbitration proceedings is generally similar to the order in proceedings in court in trial before a judge without a jury. Generally, parties will make opening statements, outlining their proof. The claimant then presents its proof (documents and witnesses), followed by the respondent's presentation. Witnesses are subject to cross-examination. There may be a rebuttal presentation from the claimant. The parties may make closing arguments.

Because of scheduling problems, it is not unusual to take testimony from witnesses out of order, when they are available. Because the arbitrator acts in more of an inquisitorial role than a jury (and many judges), it is also not unusual for an arbitrator to conduct question-and-answer sessions with counsel, throughout the proceedings, as the arbitrator focuses his or her attention on the essential issues and evidence involved in resolving the case. Thus, although the basic structure of a trial is generally preserved, arbitration hearings are often more fluid and informal than trials.

SETTING FOR THE HEARING

Where not agreed to between the parties, the location of an arbitration hearing is generally chosen by the arbitrator. Although some arbitration-sponsoring organizations offer hearing rooms as part of their service, often arbitration hearings take place in conference rooms at law offices or hotels. These settings contribute to the informal atmosphere of many arbitration hearings.

Not all arbitration proceedings are recorded. Where the stakes are small, or the parties have chosen for other reasons not to record the proceedings, the informal nature of arbitration is even further reinforced. The absence of a formal record, moreover, may make it very difficult to mount a challenge to an award. The sense, in many arbitration proceedings, is that parties will take their "best shot" to convince an arbitrator, and thereafter live with whatever result is obtained.

PRESENTATION OF EVIDENCE

The drive to conduct efficient proceedings, the informality of the setting and the extensive experience of most arbitrators generally combine to produce the rule that an arbitrator will allow almost any relevant fact into evidence, "for what it is worth." Objections based on lack of foundation or hearsay are often overruled. An arbitrator may, however, weigh such objections in determining how much value the evidence has in resolving the dispute.

For example, when a party shows that a witness is unavailable to testify, it may be possible to convince an arbitrator to receive testimony in the form of an affidavit, even though the witness testimony is technically hearsay and the opposing party will not have an opportunity to cross-examine the witness. Although the arbitrator may accept the affidavit, the arbitrator may nevertheless give it little weight (because of the hearsay and cross-examination problems). Thus, for most practitioners, in most arbitration proceedings, it is important to argue about the weight of such evidence, not its admissibility.

In the same way, objections to the form of questioning are rarely well-regarded. Although it is technically impermissible to lead a witness on direct examination, for example, many arbitrators will permit such questioning to speed the proceedings. Again, however, poor form in questioning may affect the credibility of witness and counsel, and thus diminish the weight to be accorded the testimony.

In addition to formally introduced evidence in an arbitration proceeding, arbitrators may consider their own knowledge of industry practice and the norms of commercial relationships. Because such practical experience can have an effect on the award, it will be important to consider the experience of candidates in selecting an arbitrator. The experience of the arbitrator may also affect the character of the presentation in a hearing. Where expert testimony might be required to inform a lay judge or juror about the background of an industry, an experienced arbitrator may require no such explanation. The experienced arbitrator, moreover, may be much more able to ask informed, relevant questions throughout the course of the proceedings.

CLOSING THE HEARING AND POST-HEARING BRIEFS

At the close of the hearing, the arbitrator will generally inquire as to whether the parties have any further witnesses or other evidence to present. Once the presentation of evidence is complete, requests to reopen the hearing to consider new evidence are generally not well-received.

In some arbitrations, brief closing arguments will suffice to summarize the facts and arguments of each party and to answer any remaining questions of the arbitrator. In more complicated matters, however, parties often submit post-hearing briefs, which can act as a "road map" of the evidence, and assist the arbitrator in rendering a fair award.

THE AWARD

An arbitrator's award generally must be stated in writing, and be signed by the arbitrator. Absent direction from the parties, in their agreement or in rules of the sponsoring organization, however, the arbitrator generally need not specify any findings of fact or state the reasons for the award.

The simple form of most awards can serve several purposes. Such awards can be issued promptly. They involve less arbitrator time and expense. Such awards may be less likely to engender dissatisfaction in the losing party, and may be less subject to being upset in the event of review in court. Finally, each arbitration proceeding is generally considered to be a separate, private dispute resolution proceeding. Thus, the opinion in one proceeding generally has no precedential value in another proceeding. As a result, there is less value in having a written record of an opinion in a case.

Despite the simplicity of most awards, it is important for purposes of ensuring compliance with the arbitrator's direction that the award specify all the relief that has been awarded and all claims that have been resolved. In some instances, therefore, an arbitrator may issue an award granting some relief, on some claims, and state that all other claims for relief are denied. In other instances, an arbitrator may issue an initial award, generally resolving the issues in the case, and requesting that the parties agree on the form of the final award, or make further submissions regarding the appropriate remedy.

POST-AWARD PROCEEDINGS

In some arbitration systems, such as proceedings sponsored by the International Chamber of Commerce, an award must be reviewed by an administrative official before it is issued. The administrator will review the award for form, and take steps to ensure that any remaining administrative tasks (such as the payment of fees) are completed.

In most other systems, however, the arbitrator simply issues the award, sending it to the parties by some agreed method (such as certified mail). Under the rules of many sponsoring organizations, the parties have some brief period of time in which to move to correct or amend the award. Generally, such motions are confined to matters of drafting error, mathematical miscalculation or failure to render a decision on an issue presented to the arbitrator. Requests for reconsideration on the merits of the award are generally not accepted.

DISCHARGE OF ARBITRATOR AND ARBITRATOR IMMUNITY

Generally, upon issuance of the award, and resolution of any post-award motions, the arbitrator is discharged from further service. In the event of any judicial review of the award, the arbitrator is generally not a necessary or proper party to the proceedings.

Indeed, the law in most jurisdictions treats an arbitrator as a quasi-judicial officer. In such capacity, an arbitrator is generally entitled to immunity from suit for actions taken in his or her official capacity. Such immunity, however, will not necessarily prevent an arbitrator from being subjected to subpoena or other process to obtain the testimony of the arbitrator regarding the conduct of the arbitration proceeding.

CONFIRMING AND VACATING ARBITRATION AWARDS

An arbitration award, without more, is merely a piece of paper (like a contract). The parties to an arbitration proceeding may (and often do) abide by an award without any intervention from a court. In many instances, however, it may be desirable for the prevailing party in an arbitration to petition a court to confirm the award. Confirmation of an award generally converts the award into a judgment of the court, which can be enforced with all the procedures applicable to any other judgment (attachment of assets, injunction and other remedies).

The losing party, similarly, may wish to initiate a proceeding to vacate the award, or to modify it on some grounds. Alternatively, the losing party may choose to wait until a petition to confirm the award is initiated and thereafter cross-move to vacate or modify the award.

The strategies of the parties in choosing when, where and how to move to confirm, vacate or modify an award will be affected by many of the procedural and substantive considerations outlined below.

Procedural Considerations

TIMING

Under the FAA, a petition to vacate or modify an award must be filed within three months after the award is filed or delivered. A petition to confirm an award, by contrast, may be filed within one year after the award is made. Similarly uneven periods generally apply under state statutes governing arbitration procedure.

Failure to petition a court to vacate or modify an award within the required period may constitute a waiver of the losing party's right to challenge the conduct of the arbitration proceedings. Thus, it will often be desirable to file such a petition promptly.

The prevailing party, by contrast, may choose to wait to bring a petition to confirm the award. The losing party may voluntarily comply with the award, avoiding the necessity for court proceedings. Further, if the statutory period for a petition to vacate or modify the award passes, the prevailing party may petition to confirm the award without risk of a counter-petition to vacate or modify the award. Thus, after the period for filing to vacate or modify the award has passed, a petition to confirm the award may be more readily granted.

The prevailing party, nevertheless, may choose to petition promptly for confirmation of the award. The initiation of a prompt petition may permit the prevailing party to choose the venue for the proceedings and to cast the prevailing party as the petitioner, rather than as the respondent, in court proceedings. Any response to the petition (to vacate or modify the award) would generally have to be brought as a compulsory counterclaim.

JURISDICTION, VENUE AND SERVICE OF PROCESS

The FAA does not automatically confer federal court subject matter jurisdiction for petitions to confirm, or to vacate or modify, arbitration awards. Instead, the FAA provides that "[i]f the parties in their agreement have agreed that a judgment of the court shall be entered upon the award made pursuant to arbitration," then such an application may be made. Further, in order to sustain a federal court proceeding, grounds for jurisdiction (such as diversity of citizenship between the parties) must exist. The fact that the arbitration may be subject to the FAA is generally not sufficient to establish subject matter jurisdiction in federal court. There is, however, at least some authority for the proposition that a federal court may take jurisdiction over a petition to vacate or modify an award where there has been "manifest disregard" of a federal right.

State statutes similarly establish particular grounds for proceedings in state court to confirm or vacate an award. These statutes must be consulted to make any determination of where a petition to confirm or vacate an award may be properly filed.

Proper venue must also be determined. Under federal law, unless the parties have agreed otherwise, venue to confirm, vacate or modify an award lies in the federal district where the award was rendered. The Supreme Court, however, has made clear that other bases under ordinary venue rules for civil proceedings (such as the location of the defendant) may also establish proper venue. Similar venue issues must be addressed when commencing a petition in state court.

Finally, any proceeding to confirm, vacate or modify an award requires personal jurisdiction over the opposing party and proper service of process. Generally, a petition to confirm or vacate an award is treated like an ordinary complaint to initiate civil litigation. The responding party must have some reasonable connection to the jurisdiction and must have been reasonably apprised of the commencement of the proceedings through service of process.

Given these potential problems with subject matter and personal jurisdiction, venue and service of process, parties are well-advised to address any such procedural issues in advance. Perhaps the easiest way to deal with such issues is to draft a comprehensive arbitration agreement which specifies where and how a petition to confirm or vacate an arbitration award may be initiated.

PROCEEDINGS ON THE PETITION

In general, proceedings to confirm, vacate or modify an award are meant to be brief and efficient rather than a lengthy re-litigation of issues addressed in the arbitration proceedings. In support of a petition to confirm an award, a prevailing party will typically submit copies of the award and the arbitration agreement pursuant to which the award was rendered. Unless the opposing party shows that there are grounds to vacate or modify the award, or that the petition is otherwise improper, the award will generally be confirmed without further proceedings.

Because the grounds for vacating or modifying an award generally do not permit review of the substance of the arbitration proceedings or the award, the party opposing an award often will attempt to demonstrate that, on the face of the pertinent arbitration agreement and award, some fundamental error has occurred. A court's review of an arbitration award is not the same as an appellate court's review of the record of lower court proceedings. Indeed, in many instances, there may be little record of the arbitration proceedings (no transcript or other recording) and no statement of factual findings or legal conclusions on which the award is based.

Where the error is not apparent on the face of the agreement and award, the party opposing entry of the award often must offer affidavits or other evidence demonstrating the nature of the claimed error. This evidence is generally reviewed on a very strict standard in the form of a motion for summary judgment. If the petitioner cannot show, with competent evidence on the motion for summary judgment, that some fundamental error occurred in the arbitration proceedings, the petition to vacate the award may simply be denied.

In very limited circumstances, a court may authorize brief discovery and an evidentiary hearing to resolve any disputed facts surrounding the motion to vacate or modify the award. In general, such proceedings will not involve testimony from the arbitrator. The extremely limited grounds for upsetting an award generally do not justify burdening arbitrators with the obligation to explain their actions, other than insofar as they may explain their reasoning in the course of the proceedings or in an award.

Given the strict standard for review and the limited opportunities for discovery and hearing, a party opposing entry of judgment confirming an award is generally well-advised to focus on any specific, easily proved, indisputable ground for vacating or modifying the award, rather than employ "shotgun" objections, which are likely to be rejected.

Heightened Review by Agreement

Some courts have permitted parties, by contract, to expand the scope of judicial review of an arbitration award. According to this view, arbitration is a creature of contract, and parties are free to agree to a heightened standard for review of an award.

Other courts, however, suggest that the FAA and parallel state statutes cannot be modified by agreement of the parties. According to this view, any arbitration proceeding, and any review of such a proceeding, must be conducted in accordance with governing arbitration statutes.

Even if a heightened standard for review were to be applied, there may be practical problems with such review. Parties contemplating heightened review, for example, may need to provide for recording of arbitration proceedings and should insist that the arbitrator provide a full statement of reasons for an award. The parties may also wish to choose a standard of review that will be familiar to a court, such as the "substantial evidence" or "clearly erroneous" standards that might be applied to review of the decisions of an administrative agency.

Substantive Issues

LIMITED REVIEW GENERALLY

One of the attractions of arbitration for many parties is its relative finality. Unlike ordinary civil proceedings, where an automatic right of appeal and review of the record at trial are standard, one basic tenet of arbitration is that judicial review of an arbitration award should be limited. Thus, in general, courts apply a presumption in favor of the enforcement of arbitration awards, and will upset such awards only on the grounds set forth in the FAA and parallel state statutes. Indeed, the FAA and parallel statutes generally provide that, unless a party shows that grounds exist to vacate or modify an award, the award must be enforced.

Consistent with such limited review, it is often said that the function of a court in reviewing an arbitration award is not to assess the merits of the arbitrator's decision. Mere error of law or fact will not suffice to upset an award. Similarly, challenges based on insufficiency of evidence are likely to fail. Interpretation of the underlying contract, moreover, is ordinarily a matter committed to the discretion of the arbitrator. Even where a court might reach a different conclusion on its own, an arbitration award generally must be enforced.

The rationale for limited judicial review arises from the nature of arbitration itself. As noted, an essential part of the bargain in an arbitration agreement is the choice of a speedy, less expensive and more final process for dispute resolution. Because arbitration proceedings are private, voluntary functions, moreover, there is not the same concern for due process that arises in a public dispute resolution system. In addition, arbitration proceedings are often not recorded, and arbitration awards often lack any statement of reasons; thus, the ability of courts to review arbitration awards is inherently limited. Finally, courts acknowledge that Congress and state legislatures have expressed public policy choices concerning the scope of judicial review of arbitration awards. The arbitration statutes they have produced aim to address serious, fundamental errors in arbitration proceedings, but to avoid the expensive, lengthy appeals process that can arise in ordinary civil litigation.

Despite this presumption in favor of limited review of arbitration awards, a court will vacate or modify an award where a statutory ground for upsetting an award exists. Applicable arbitration law (the FAA and/or parallel state statutes) must be consulted to determine the specific grounds for review. The remainder of this section discusses the grounds for review found in most such statutes.

AWARD IN EXCESS OF ARBITRATOR'S POWERS

Because arbitrators draw their dispute resolution authority from the agreement of the parties, an award in excess of that authority may be vacated. Thus, if an arbitrator has been given one task (to establish a valuation on property, for example) and engages in another task (awarding damages, for example), the award may be vacated as in excess of the arbitrator's powers. Similarly, an arbitrator's *sua sponte* award on claims that were not presented by any party may be vacated. Further, where an arbitrator awards relief against a party that is not properly subject to arbitration (for lack of agreement to arbitrate, for example), the award may be vacated.

Despite these potential grounds for vacating an award, courts often consider whether a party has waived such objections by participating in an arbitration proceeding without objection. Where objections are not properly lodged during the course of an arbitration proceeding, a court may find that, even though the arbitrator did not have authority under the original arbitration agreement, such authority may be implied from the conduct of the arbitration proceeding without objection from the parties.

An issue may arise regarding public policy limits on arbitration. Certain subjects (criminal matters, for example) are obviously beyond the power of arbitrators to resolve. Many other subjects (antitrust, securities law and RICO claims, for example), which were formerly considered beyond the power of arbitrators to resolve, are now recognized as appropriate for arbitration. Certain other subjects (EEO claims and debtor/creditor issues where a bankruptcy case is pending, for example) may, or may not, be subject to arbitration depending on the circumstances of the case and the view of the individual judge reviewing the arbitration award or the position of the appellate courts in that state or circuit.

LIMITS ON REMEDIES: PUNITIVE DAMAGES AND ATTORNEYS' FEES

The question of whether an award exceeds an arbitrator's powers includes the question of the scope of remedies that an arbitrator may award. Ordinarily, any remedy that a judge or jury might award is also proper for an arbitrator. Indeed, in certain instances, an arbitrator may award relief (a mandatory license in an intellectual property dispute, for example) that might not be available in court.

Nevertheless, an arbitrator generally may not grant some forms of relief (such as an award of punitive damages or attorneys' fees) without specific authority. Punitive damage awards by arbitrators have been particularly problematic, for a number of reasons.

Punitive damages, unlike compensatory damages, are expressly meant to serve a public purpose: deterring egregiously wrongful behavior. Arbitration tribunals, however, are distinctly private entities. Thus, some courts have suggested that arbitrators should not be permitted to award punitive damages. The processes of arbitration (limited discovery, no jury trial) may also appear inappropriate as predicates for punitive damage awards.

Other courts have suggested that, since an arbitrator is generally qualified to award any form of relief that might be available from a court, an arbitrator should be permitted to award punitive damages. In still other jurisdictions, the rule appears to be that an arbitrator may grant punitive damages, but only where the parties have expressly granted the arbitrator authority to render such an award.

State legislatures in some instances have placed express limits on the remedial powers of arbitrators. In at least one state, for example, arbitrators are prohibited by statute from awarding attorneys' fees. Such statutory limits on an arbitrator's remedial powers are probably not preempted by the FAA, which contains no express provisions on such matters as attorneys' fees or punitive damages.

The rules of a sponsoring organization may expressly grant an arbitrator authority to award relief, such as attorneys' fees to the prevailing party. Because agreement to arbitrate under the auspices of a sponsoring organization generally involves agreement to follow the rules of that sponsoring organization, parties must be careful to examine the rules to determine whether an arbitrator may have been granted remedial powers, such as the power to award attorneys' fees, that might not otherwise be available in litigation. To avoid any uncertainty about the powers of an arbitrator, it is generally preferable for parties to draft a specific arbitration agreement and to be clear during the course of the proceedings as to what powers they expect the arbitrator to exercise.

MANIFEST DISREGARD OF LAW

Although there is no express provision in the FAA that permits a court to vacate an arbitration award for error of law, some courts have suggested that an award may be vacated where it is in "manifest disregard" of law. Consistent with the general presumption of regularity of arbitration, and deferential review of awards, however, this standard is strictly applied. In effect, by permitting *vacatur* of an award for manifest disregard of law, courts have established a fail-safe mechanism, aimed at preventing egregiously lawless decisions by an arbitrator.

In articulating the "manifest disregard" standard, courts often refer to both the clarity and the importance of the controlling law. That is, where the law disregarded by the arbitrator is infused with a public character of long-standing and well-defined nature, *vacatur* is more likely. Where the law or common law rule is of a more mundane nature, or where there is a split in authority as to the meaning of the law, the arbitrator's choice to disregard the law may be more tolerable to the courts. Where the arbitrator merely chooses between two possible rules of law, moreover, such a choice will almost never be second-guessed by a court, even if the award is not what the court might have granted in the first instance.

The disregard of law, moreover, must be "manifest." A flat statement by an arbitrator that "I know the controlling law, but I choose not to follow the law," will rarely (if ever) appear in a record of arbitration. As a result, disregard of law must be inferred from the circumstances of the proceedings. Again, because of the inherent limits in court review of an arbitration proceeding (where there may be no transcript, and often only a terse statement of award), courts will not routinely take up a party's invitation to search for purported manifest disregard of law by an arbitrator. The manifest disregard standard is, instead, largely a check against extreme, obvious arbitrator lawlessness.

FRAUD AND CORRUPTION

The fraud and corruption grounds for vacating an arbitration award essentially concern fundamental improprieties in the conduct of an arbitration. Thus, for example, where the arbitrator harbors some bias against one of the parties, such that a fair award may be impossible, the award may be vacated. Yet, because a claim of bias may be relatively easy to make, and could conceivably result in undue intrusion into the arbitration process, courts generally apply this ground for review of an award strictly. If the arbitrator was selected through ordinary processes of disclosure and challenge for potential conflicts or bias, and no challenges were lodged, the award will generally be sustained. An arbitrator's failure to disclose conflicts or bias, or an arbitrator's failure to disqualify himself after proper challenge, however, may result in *vacatur* of the award.

Similarly, gross improprieties during the course of the arbitration hearing may be grounds for vacating an award. Thus, in general, *ex parte* contacts between an arbitrator and a party (or its representative) are improper because the other party is not aware of potential influence on the arbitrator's decision and has no opportunity to respond. Again, however, courts apply this ground for overturning an award strictly. Incidental communication between an arbitrator and a party is generally not an automatic ground for *vacatur* of an award.

Where the purported fraud precedes the arbitration, moreover, a court will generally find that the issue is for the arbitrator alone to resolve. Thus, for example, where one party claims that a contract was induced by fraud, the claim goes to the merits of the dispute, rather than the conduct of the arbitration itself.

LACK OF OPPORTUNITY TO PRESENT A PARTY'S CASE

The FAA and parallel state statutes generally require that an arbitrator give a party an opportunity to present evidence that is material to its case. Similarly, where good cause is shown, an arbitrator must postpone a hearing in order to give a party an opportunity to present its evidence.

This general due process directive is not usually read expansively, however. An arbitrator enjoys substantial discretion to conduct arbitration proceedings in an efficient manner. An arbitrator, moreover, enjoys similar discretion in determining what issues are material in the arbitration, and in applying rules of evidence. Indeed, it is often suggested that ordinary rules of evidence need not be applied in arbitration.

Despite this broad discretion, the rule requiring an opportunity for a hearing acts as a kind of fail-safe against abuse of the arbitration process. An arbitrator could not simply declare that he has reached a decision without hearing from the parties. Nor could an arbitrator state that he will hear evidence and argument from one side, but not the other.

The opportunity to be heard does not necessarily mean that a hearing will be conducted. It is quite possible to obtain a default award through arbitration. Where the defaulting party has been given adequate notice of the proceedings, and the proponent of the award makes some minimal showing of the basis for an award, the award may be granted even if the other party does not appear. Further, it is possible for parties to agree that no evidentiary hearing is required in order to resolve a dispute. In that event, the arbitrator may decide the matter on a paper record.

FAILURE TO FOLLOW AGREED UPON PROCEDURES

Because an arbitrator's powers are generally derived from the agreement of the parties to a dispute, and because parties are generally free to adopt the procedures for arbitration that they deem fit, an award made in blatant disregard of the procedures agreed to between the parties arguably exceeds the arbitrator's powers.

Thus, for example, if the parties had agreed that the Federal Rules of Evidence should be strictly applied in the arbitration proceedings, and an arbitrator admitted extensive hearsay evidence, the award might be subject to *vacatur.* This kind of objection to an award might also arise where parties choose the arbitration rules of a particular sponsoring organization, and the arbitrator fails to follow those rules.

The rules of most sponsoring organizations, however, grant substantial discretion to arbitrators in the conduct of proceedings. As a result, unless parties are very specific in their arbitration agreement about the procedures they expect an arbitrator to follow, and unless the arbitrator conducts the proceedings in disregard of those agreed upon procedures, there may be little chance of *vacatur* of the award by a court.

FAILURE TO RULE ON ISSUES PRESENTED

Referral of claims to arbitration generally precludes a party from pursuing those same claims in court. As a result, part of the benefit of the bargain for arbitration is the ability to obtain review from the arbitrator of all issues presented.

Where an arbitrator's award does not rule on all issues presented, technically it is not final, and thus a petition to confirm the award is not ripe. In such a situation, a court might vacate the award as not final, with directions that the parties seek a final award from the arbitrator.

Despite this potential objection to an award, there is generally a presumption that, unless the arbitrator expressly reserves certain issues (e.g., costs, fees or interest), the award is to be considered final, and thus subject to enforcement, *vacatur* or modification. Some arbitrators, moreover, will enter an award that states that all claims not specifically addressed in the award are denied. Moreover, certain non-final awards (such as an award of preliminary relief) may be considered final for purposes of enforcement of the award, even though further proceedings are contemplated.

CORRECTION OF MISTAKES

The FAA and parallel state statutes generally permit courts to correct evident mistakes in an award. Where an arbitrator has miscalculated interest on an award, for example, the interest could be recomputed by a court and the award enforced, as modified.

Other evident defects in the form of an award (such as misidentification of parties in the proceeding or the property that is the subject of the dispute) may also be corrected. Where the court is uncertain about whether a mistake has been made, however, the better course may be to vacate the award, with direction to obtain a clearer award from the arbitrator.

Post-Review Proceedings

In the simplest of circumstances, if an award is issued by an arbitrator and a petition to confirm the award is granted by a court, the award becomes a judgment, or order, of the court. The parties are required to comply with the judgment, as they would be required to comply with any other court order. If one of the parties fails to comply, moreover, the judgment may be enforced, using any of the ordinary powers of a court to enforce an order.

Difficulties may arise, however, where something other than a simple order of enforcement is entered. If, for example, an award is vacated, in whole or in part, there may be a need for further proceedings (such as an additional evidentiary hearing, or further rulings on issues that were not properly considered in connection with the arbitrator's award). A court reviewing an arbitration award, however, generally has no authority to conduct such hearings, or to rule on the merits of such issues; these functions are within the province of the arbitrator.

In ordinary civil litigation, the remedy in such circumstances would be for the reviewing court to remand the matter to a trial court for further proceedings. In general, however, an arbitrator's duties are discharged upon the issuance of an award. Thus, if further arbitration proceedings are required, the parties may need to make arrangements either to reconstitute the original arbitration tribunal or to establish a new tribunal to conduct further proceedings. The inconvenience and expense involved in setting up and conducting such further proceedings may be one reason that courts are reluctant to vacate an arbitration award.

CLAIM AND ISSUE PRECLUSION

The doctrines of claim and issue preclusion (*res judicata* and collateral estoppel) are generally applied to bar relitigation of claims and issues resolved by arbitration. Thus, if a party were to bring a claim on a contract to arbitration, and the arbitrator rendered an award rejecting the claim, the party generally could not initiate a lawsuit on the same contract claim in court. Similarly, if an arbitrator were to render an award determining that a contract had been voided by the actions of a party, the arbitrator's award on that issue would generally be binding on the parties in the event that another dispute arose out of that contract. In each instance, a court proceeding might be initiated seeking to vacate the original arbitration award, but a new suit that ignored the results of the earlier arbitration proceeding could not be brought. Thus, the ordinary mechanisms for review of an arbitration award generally cannot be skirted by initiating collateral litigation after an award is rendered.

The application of the claim and issue preclusion concepts to arbitration, however, often can be more complex than these simple illustrations suggest. For example, where an arbitration agreement is narrowly written, such that certain claims are not included within the matters submitted to the arbitrator, an arbitration award may not have a preclusive effect. Similarly, where a court concludes that, as a matter of public policy, arbitration of certain issues is inappropriate, preclusive effects may be avoided.

Further, where the question is whether a particular issue was resolved in an arbitration proceeding, the lack of a complete record of such a proceeding may make analysis difficult. A bare award rendering a decision in favor of one party, without a statement of reasons, may not suffice to confirm how the arbitrator arrived at the decision and what issues were resolved in the process. Thus, the preclusive effect of the award may be limited.

Chapter 8

INTERNATIONAL ARBITRATION

International arbitration has developed over the past century as a significant method of resolving disputes between parties of multiple nationalities. Although many commentators suggest that speed and economy are the chief advantages of international arbitration, the reality is that international arbitration is often most desirable simply because of the problems it avoids.

Absent an agreement providing for arbitration of disputes, parties in conflict will often have an incentive to "race to the courthouse" in their home countries. This incentive may include the desire to maximize one's own convenience in litigation, and to operate in a familiar system, where the rules, the judges and the lawyers are well known. If there is no agreement to arbitrate, both parties may commence actions in their home courts, and the judges in those courts will be required to decide whether both actions can go forward, and if not, which one should proceed. Even if only one action is filed, most likely there will be arguments on *forum non conveniens,* jurisdiction, service of process and other issues that often arise in conventional litigation. Ultimately, there may be relitigation of issues when a party seeks to enforce a judgment obtained in its home jurisdiction by way of a second action in the other party's home jurisdiction.

All of this preliminary and ancillary litigation can take time, cost a great deal of money, and reduce the certainty of dispute resolution. Parties involved in long-term contractual relationships (such as joint ventures) may require swift and certain answers to the questions surrounding their contract, which protracted procedural fights will not produce. Even a choice of forum provision in a contract will not necessarily ensure that such procedural skirmishing is avoided. There is no universal agreement on the enforceability of such clauses. Choice of an arbitral forum, by contrast, is governed by a nearly universal international convention, and by well-developed norms for the conduct of international arbitration.

The New York Convention

In 1958, the United Nations promulgated the Convention on the Recognition and Enforcement of Foreign Arbitral Awards. This multilateral treaty is generally known as the "New York Convention" because of its creation at the United Nations in New York City. The New York Convention has been ratified by more than 100 countries, including virtually every major commercial nation. Significant provisions of the Convention are summarized below.

APPLICABILITY

The Convention applies to recognition and enforcement in one nation's courts of an arbitral award made in another nation. Each signatory of the Convention, moreover, may designate other types of arbitral awards that will be considered not "domestic" for purposes of applying the Convention. In addition, each nation may provide that it will only apply the Convention to awards made in the territory of another signatory nation. Nations may also specify that the Convention will only be applied to disputes arising out of relationships that are considered "commercial" under the laws of that nation.

COMPELLING ARBITRATION

The Convention provides that each signatory nation must recognize an "agreement in writing" to submit to arbitration. The Convention broadly defines an "agreement in writing" to include any exchange of letters or telegrams evidencing such an agreement to arbitrate.

The Convention provides that the courts of a signatory nation must, if an arbitration agreement covers the subject matter of a pending dispute, "refer the parties to arbitration." This provision, however, is not self-executing. One of the parties must request that the matter be referred to arbitration. Further, if a court finds that the agreement is "null and void, inoperative or incapable of being performed," it will not be enforced.

ENFORCING AWARDS

The Convention sets forth the broad principle that each signatory nation must recognize and enforce arbitral awards. Although rules of procedure may vary in the courts of individual signatory nations, no nation may impose "substantially more onerous conditions or higher fees" for the recognition and enforcement of foreign arbitral awards than are imposed on the recognition and enforcement of domestic awards.

Recognition and enforcement of a foreign arbitral award is generally made simple by the Convention. The proponent of the award need only show: (a) a duly authenticated award, or certified copy; (b) the arbitration agreement on which the arbitration proceeding and award were founded; and (c) if either of such documents (the agreement or the award) is in a language other than the official language of the nation where recognition is sought, certified translations of such documents.

Recognition and enforcement may be refused only under limited circumstances. The party opposing enforcement may attempt to show: (a) that the arbitration agreement was not valid; (b) that the party was not given proper notice of the appointment of an arbitrator or the arbitration proceeding, or was otherwise unable to present its case; (c) that the award deals with a dispute not covered by the arbitration agreement (except that decisions properly subject to the arbitration agreement may be recognized even though the remainder of the award is not recognized); (d) that the composition of the tribunal or the conduct of the proceedings was not in accordance with the agreement of the parties or the law of the place where the arbitration took place; or (e) that the award is under consideration by, or has been set aside by, a court in the country where the award was made. When this last argument is invoked, a court may adjourn its decision on enforcement until the court in the nation where the award was made has an opportunity to rule.

The Convention also embodies an amorphous general exception to enforcement where, under the law of the country in which recognition and enforcement is sought, the subject matter of the dispute is not capable of settlement by arbitration, or recognition or enforcement of the award would be contrary to that country's public policy. Despite the potential for that general exception to swallow the rule of the Convention, in practice most nations (including the United States) have applied the exception for subject matter inarbitrability or public policy concerns only on narrow, rare grounds.

OTHER TREATIES

The New York Convention does not affect the validity of any other multilateral or bilateral treaties concerning arbitration. The Convention, however, is the most universal of all such treaties, and it is fair to say that the Convention is the foundation on which all modern international arbitration rests.

The Federal Arbitration Act

Despite its near universal recognition today, the New York Convention was not well-received in the United States at the time of its introduction in 1958. The American response was based largely on a traditional antipathy to participation in entangling international regulation, and corresponding relinquishment of national legal autonomy. By 1970, however, the American attitude had changed, and the United States ratified the Convention.

The Convention, as a treaty, became the "supreme law of the land," binding on courts in the United States just as the Constitution and federal laws are binding. To implement the Convention, in 1970, Congress enacted amendments to the Federal Arbitration Act. These amendments, Chapter Two of the FAA, basically provide that the New York Convention is enforceable in United States courts.

The FAA, however, provides that the United States will only recognize the application of the Convention to "commercial" disputes. Further, the FAA defines "foreign" arbitral awards to exclude any dispute that is entirely between citizens of the United States, unless the dispute involves property located abroad, or an agreement envisages performance or enforcement abroad, or has some other "reasonable relation" to one or more foreign nations.

The FAA provides for federal court subject matter jurisdiction over actions governed by the Convention. If such an action is brought in a state court, it may be removed to federal court.

The FAA specifies that a court, pursuant to the Convention, may compel arbitration in accordance with the parties' agreement, whether the arbitration is to be conducted inside or outside the United States. The court may also appoint arbitrators in accordance with the provisions of the parties' agreement.

The FAA permits any party to an arbitration agreement to seek an order confirming an arbitration award. Such an application must be made within three years of the date that the award is made. The court must confirm the award unless it finds one of the grounds for refusal or deferral of recognition specified in the Convention.

The FAA provides that, to the extent that the provisions of the Convention are not in conflict with them, the basic procedures set forth in Chapter One of the FAA will govern in actions pursuant to the Convention. Thus, for example, Chapter One of the FAA specifies that actions pursuant to the FAA will be handled expeditiously, using the procedure for motion practice. That provision is not inconsistent with the Convention (which says nothing on the subject).

Sample Arbitration Rules

Several major arbitration-sponsoring institutions offer rules and administrative resources for purposes of conducting an international arbitration. One of the oldest (established in 1923), and most widely-recognized, is the International Chamber of Commerce (ICC), headquartered in Paris. The ICC Rules are specifically designed for international arbitration, and encompass most of the procedures that are typical in international arbitration. Summarized below are some of the essential elements of the ICC Rules.

CENTRAL ADMINISTRATION

One unique element of ICC practice is the central role played by the ICC International Court of Arbitration in the administration of arbitral cases. The ICC and its "Court" are private institutions. The ICC Court is designed to provide diverse, world-wide input into the construction and implementation of ICC Rules, and the oversight of arbitration proceedings. The Court currently includes some sixty-five members, from more than fifty-five countries.

The Court itself does not settle disputes. Indeed, members of the Court cannot act as arbitrators or as counsel in cases submitted to ICC arbitration. Instead, the Court's function is to ensure the effective application of the ICC Rules. The Court is generally involved in appointment and confirmation of arbitrators, and is always involved in review of draft awards prior to their issuance.

CHOOSING ARBITRATORS

The norm in ICC arbitration proceedings (which tend to be large, commercial disputes) is for the use of three arbitrators, one selected by each of the parties, with the final arbitrator either selected by the first two, or by the ICC Court. The third arbitrator serves as the "chairman" of the tribunal. If the parties do not provide a method of selecting arbitrators, the Court will make the selection, and will choose a single arbitrator unless the circumstances of the dispute otherwise warrant a three-member tribunal.

The ICC Rules generally require that all arbitrators remain independent of the parties involved in the arbitration. All arbitrators, whether appointed by the parties or the Court, must file either a statement of independence, or a "qualified" statement of independence, which itemizes potential limitations on independence. The Court will confirm arbitrators only after giving the parties an opportunity to object on independence (and other) grounds. A sole arbitrator or chairman ordinarily must be a chosen from a country other than the countries of which the parties are nationals (unless the circumstances otherwise dictate, and no party objects).

WRITTEN SUBMISSIONS

Following a largely European tradition, ICC arbitration often proceeds with relatively detailed pleadings and exchange of documents in connection with those pleadings before (or in substitution for) any oral hearing of testimony. Typically, the claimant begins the proceedings by filing a request for arbitration, accompanied by any relevant agreements (including any agreement submitting to arbitration). The respondent then files an answer to the request, coupled with any counterclaims and relevant agreements. A reply may be filed on any counterclaims.

Soon after its appointment by the ICC Court, the arbitration tribunal is required to draw up "terms of reference," which include summaries of claims and defenses, and a list of issues to be determined. The terms of reference are typically drafted in consultation with the parties, and signed by the parties, and thus constitute a separate agreement on submission of the dispute to arbitration. If the terms of reference are not signed, the ICC Court will review and approve them, and the arbitration will proceed.

The ICC Rules provide that a tribunal will proceed "within as short a time as possible" to establish the facts of the case by all "appropriate" means. The Rules contemplate that the parties will make written submissions to the tribunal, including all documents to be relied upon in supporting claims and defenses, before the tribunal determines whether and how to hear oral submissions from the parties. Typically, a tribunal will establish a pre-hearing briefing schedule, and the parties will expend considerable effort in submitting briefs and supporting documentation before any oral hearing is conducted.

ADDITIONAL PROCEEDINGS

The ICC Rules give a tribunal considerable discretion in determining how to conduct oral hearings. The tribunal may, after consultation with the parties, appoint one or more experts to assist the tribunal in evaluating technical issues in the case. In that event, the tribunal-appointed expert typically will submit a report, and be available for cross-examination.

The parties may also offer their own expert and fact witnesses for testimony. The Rules state that each party shall be given a "reasonable opportunity" to present its case, but also recognize that the tribunal shall be in "full charge" of any hearings. When the tribunal is satisfied that the parties have been given a reasonable opportunity to make their submissions, the tribunal will declare the proceedings closed.

THE AWARD

The ICC Rules generally require that any award must be rendered within six months of the date on which the terms of reference are signed. This time limit may be extended by the ICC Court on request from the tribunal. Any award must state the "reasons" for the tribunal's decision, although the scope of such reasons is a matter for the discretion of each tribunal. Awards are made by majority decision. Before an award is rendered, it must be submitted in draft form to the ICC Court for review. The Court may make modifications as to form, and may also draw the tribunal's attention to matters of substance (although the substantive decision is always a matter for the tribunal alone).

Cross-Cultural Perspectives

The ICC is only one of many organizations that sponsor international arbitration proceedings. Although an arbitration sponsored by a particular organization may be conducted virtually anywhere in the world, it is not unusual for European parties and counsel to favor ICC proceedings (administered from Paris); American parties and counsel to favor American Arbitration Association proceedings (administered from New York); and English parties to favor proceedings sponsored by the London Court of International Arbitration (also a private institution, headquartered in London).

International arbitration proceedings, moreover, often involve parties, lawyers and arbitrators with widely varying experiences and views on procedure for litigation and dispute resolution. The American system of litigation, involving free-ranging discovery and often lengthy hearings, is at one extreme. The Continental system, involving very limited (if any) discovery and limited in-person hearings is at the other extreme. The English system, involving some document discovery but no pre-trial depositions, with often extensive cross-examination at hearings, is somewhere in between.

Frequently, arbitration agreements concerning international transactions do not specify whether (and how much) discovery and trial-type process will be allowed. The rules of sponsoring organizations, moreover, provide only limited guidance on how proceedings are to be conducted. As a result, the predilections of the arbitrators, and the necessities of the situation, will determine what discovery and trial procedures are followed.

THE AMERICAN APPROACH

American lawyers generally expect to be able to obtain from their adversaries all documents relevant to a dispute, not just those offered in evidence by the opposition, and to receive those documents well before trial. American lawyers are also accustomed to obtaining deposition testimony from witnesses connected with the parties, and even third parties, irrespective of whether such witnesses are willing to testify voluntarily. The breadth of potential discovery is generally quite wide, bounded only by generous limits of relevance and undue burden. Ancillary procedures for written interrogatories, requests for admissions and inspection of relevant places and things are also commonly used.

For American lawyers, the point of this broad-ranging discovery is to gather materials both to help make their case at trial and to help prepare for cross-examination of an adversary's witnesses at trial. The trial is the critical ground for making one's case, and for exposing weaknesses in the other side's case. Even in commercial cases involving extensive documentation, witness credibility may be tested through cross-examination, using (among other things) documents and answers to deposition questions.

THE ENGLISH APPROACH

The English tradition is similar to the American, except that it generally does not permit pre-trial interrogation of witnesses and does not permit pre-trial discovery of documents from third parties. It does, however, afford ample opportunity for parties to obtain relevant documents from one another in advance of trial. Like the American system, the English system incorporates cross-examination of witnesses, and prizes this practice as a way of exposing and correcting unreliable testimony.

Differences between the American and English systems of discovery and trial should not be underestimated, however. English lawyers are accustomed to conducting a painstaking cross-examination of a witness' statement in front of a judge, while American lawyers are accustomed to preparing a cross-examination that draws from both the witness' discovery deposition and his oral examination. Moreover, the American lawyer, more than an English counterpart, must appeal to a jury. These differences affect the character of pre-trial discovery.

Because the English advocate can expect a free-ranging opportunity to conduct cross-examination at trial, and generally will not risk boring a jury by essentially conducting discovery as part of the trial, pre-trial discovery expectations are reduced. Although discovery is considered an essential feature of the English adversary system, discovery in England has never followed the wide-ranging approach embodied in the American system. Under the English system, for example, a document requested must be shown to be relevant to the dispute; wide-ranging "fishing" discovery is not permissible.

THE CONTINENTAL APPROACH

Commercial law cases in continental Europe generally place primary emphasis on documents. The principal method of production of evidence is through the exchange, before hearing, of pleadings and briefs, which typically annex the documents upon which each party's position is founded. Witnesses, if any, are heard only after exchanges of pleadings and documents.

The Continental system generally does not permit pre-hearing deposition of witnesses. Even when hearings are permitted, testimony is often restricted. Continental lawyers generally do not see much point in witness examination that adds nothing to information already in documents before the court. Further, the Continental system finds cross-examination in the English and American styles tedious, burdensome, and often unfair to the witness. The point of cross-examination, in the Continental system, is more to adduce facts that are not otherwise available from the documents, to aid the court in understanding the documents, and to help determine which of the documents may be more reliable than the others. Often, Continental judges will take it upon themselves, in inquisitorial fashion, to ask these kinds of questions of the witnesses directly.

Where pre-hearing discovery is taken in the Continental system, a judge's intervention is required. Discovery does not automatically follow from the request from one party for information from the other. Some form of showing that a document exists, and that it is relevant to the proceeding, must be made. A Continental jurist, moreover, generally considers it his duty to inquire into the case, and thus may, on his own motion, call for the production of documents, order an expert opinion, or conduct an inspection or site visit.

The procedural laws and related practices in the Continental European countries are not all identical. There are often as many differences as similarities between these various systems. Yet, it may be fairly said that Continental lawyers and judges abhor the kind of wasteful, costly and potentially abusive discovery practices they associate with the American system.

Discovery and Hearing Rules of Major Arbitration Organizations

The rules of most major arbitration-sponsoring organizations do not generally seek to establish a comprehensive regime of arbitral procedures. The procedures for pre-hearing discovery, in particular, are frequently outlined only in very general terms. Despite the vagueness of the rules, the major sponsoring organizations reflect, at least to some degree, the legal systems from which they have grown.

As previously explained, the rules of the ICC provide that an arbitral tribunal shall "proceed within as short a time as possible to establish the facts of the case by all appropriate means." The ICC Rules contemplate construction of "terms of reference," in which the parties agree (among other things) upon the "particulars of the applicable procedural rules" for the case. Typically, at or before the conference where the terms of reference are finalized, the parties will agree on issues pertaining to the mode of discovery in the case.

Despite these flexible directives, the ICC system of arbitration generally follows a Continental approach to procedure. The parties generally define the issues in the case by exchanging pleadings, together with the contract(s) at issue and other relevant documents. The arbitral tribunal may decide to hear witnesses, appoint experts, or call for the production of specific documents necessary to decide the case, but may also (in the absence of a request for a hearing) decide the case solely on the documents submitted by the parties.

Similarly, the rules of the London Court of International Arbitration (LCIA) provide that arbitral tribunals have the "widest discretion" to discharge their duties as necessary for the "fair, efficient and expeditious conduct" of an arbitration proceeding. Parties are also encouraged to agree upon the method by which their individual arbitration proceedings will be conducted, and arbitrators are generally directed to "adopt procedures suitable to the circumstances of the arbitration."

As in the ICC rules, the LCIA rules contemplate an exchange of pleadings, coupled with copies of "essential documents." The LCIA rules, however, are much more explicit in providing that an arbitral tribunal may order a party to produce (to the tribunal and other parties) "any documents or classes of documents in their possession, custody or power which the Arbitral Tribunal determines to be relevant." The rules also contemplate appointment of experts, who report to the tribunal. Parties may be required to provide relevant documents and other information to such experts. The LCIA rules, however, do not provide for any pre-hearing deposition of witnesses.

The international arbitration rules of the American Arbitration Association (AAA) provide that a tribunal may, within the bounds of fairness and equality of treatment, "conduct the arbitration in whatever manner it considers appropriate." Unlike the ICC and LCIA rules, the AAA rules do not expressly contemplate the exchange of documents along with the pleadings in the case. Instead, the AAA rules generally provide that a tribunal may order a party to identify the documents and other evidence on which it relies in support of its claims, and may order parties to produce "other documents, exhibits or other evidence it deems necessary or appropriate." The AAA rules also permit appointment of experts who report to the tribunal, and who may require a party to produce any relevant documents that the experts may require. Under the FAA and parallel state statutes, moreover, AAA arbitration proceedings conducted in the United States may also involve production of evidence from third parties. Despite this broader authority, the AAA rules do not generally contemplate pre-hearing deposition of parties or other witnesses.

TOWARD A SYNTHESIS OF PROCEDURES

Despite the wide theoretical gaps between the American, English and Continental systems of discovery and hearing, and despite the disparities in rules for the major sponsoring organizations, over the past thirty or more years a consensus has developed as to certain core principles regarding procedures in international arbitration. These basic principles are not rules, *per se,* but rather standards of practice that have come to be widely accepted, largely because of real constraints imposed by the nature of international arbitration proceedings. Arbitrators may feel free to depart from these principles, in appropriate circumstances, but there must be some articulated reason why the basic principles should not be applied.

First, the primary source of information for resolution of international commercial arbitration disputes is the documentary evidence submitted by the parties. Typically, such documents are produced by the parties as part of the process of pleading and briefing their cases, before any oral hearing is conducted. This principle follows, in part, from the nature of international commercial disputes. Given the distances that parties, witnesses, lawyers and arbitrators often must travel to participate in oral hearings, and the cost and burden associated with such hearings, oral hearings must be as abbreviated as possible. Thus, where relevant documents can be examined well before such hearings, and their meaning largely explicated without testimony, arbitrators expect parties in international arbitration to identify and produce relevant documents (to the extent that they support a party's case) voluntarily, and well in advance of any hearing. Parties have an incentive to produce such documents voluntarily, moreover, as a consequence of the rule, generally applied in international arbitration, that "he who asserts a fact must prove it."

Second, it is virtually unheard of for arbitrators in international arbitration disputes to order pre-hearing depositions. This principle follows from the primary emphasis on documents, and from the expectation that any oral hearings will be abbreviated, such that pre-hearing depositions, intended to provide fodder for cross-examination at the hearing, are not appropriate.

Although some pre-hearing discovery of an adversary's documents may be permitted, the proponent of the discovery request must make some showing that the documents exist, that they are in the possession of the adversary, and that they are necessary to a fair decision in the case. This principle recognizes that arbitration proceedings should be as efficient and swift as possible, and that involvement of arbitrators in discovery disputes will detract from those purposes. Further, this principle coincides neatly with the preferred sanction for failure to produce an essential document: an "adverse inference," i.e., the possibility that the tribunal will conclude that a relevant document, if produced, would have been detrimental to the intransigent party.

As may be seen, these basic principles are generally rather favorable to the Continental practitioner. Even with limited discovery, however, a skillful English or American practitioner may, in the limited time provided for oral hearing, make effective use of cross-examination and testimony from his own witnesses and experts. The essential imperative for such practitioners is to find a way to be focused and brief, both in asking for any discovery and in conducting any oral hearing.

There are certain inherent barriers that probably foreclose, at least for the foreseeable future, development of a truly a-national, comprehensive set of rules for international commercial arbitration, including rules of discovery.

First, each arbitral tribunal tends to be a law unto itself. The rules adopted and applied for the occasion are to a large degree determined by the cultural background of the members of the tribunal. Most international arbitrators are lawyers or jurists, who prefer to apply procedures with which they are familiar.

Second, there are few external constraints on the operation of international arbitral tribunals. Although a disappointed party may attempt to challenge an award based on the assertion that denial of discovery, or an opportunity to put particular questions by cross-examination, made him unable to present his case, in practice failure to follow a specific requested practice can almost never be the basis for a successful challenge to an award. Further, to the extent that review of awards involves discovery and hearing procedure issues, that review is conducted in courts around the globe, with judges applying their own views of what constitutes fundamental fairness.

Finally, to some extent, diversity in procedures for international commercial arbitration is desirable. In some international arbitrations it may be obvious, from the nationality of the parties, the law of the contract, the place of the arbitration or other factors that problems of discovery and proof should be resolved using a Continental, English or American system. Thus, a strict one-size-fits-all standard is neither necessary nor desirable.

LABOR, EMPLOYMENT, CONSUMER AND SECURITIES ARBITRATION

Although there can be great variety in the conduct of commercial arbitration proceedings, in general the law and rules governing such proceedings are relatively consistent. The basic structure of an arbitration proceeding may be preserved outside the commercial arbitration arena as well. Cases involving labor, employment, consumer and securities arbitration, however, often can introduce novel concepts and problems not ordinarily seen in commercial arbitration. This chapter summarizes some of the more distinctive elements of these sometimes novel proceedings.

Labor Arbitration

SOURCES OF LAW

In 1935, Congress enacted the Wagner Act, which recognized that the proper role for unions was to bargain collectively with employers for contracts covering wages, hours and other terms and conditions of employment. The Wagner Act implicitly assumed that collective bargaining agreements were binding and enforceable, but the Act contained no specific mechanism for enforcement. In 1947, Congress enacted the Labor Management

Relations Act, which provides for federal court jurisdiction for purposes of enforcing collective bargaining agreements.

Courts have held that the power to enforce a collective bargaining agreement includes the power to enforce an arbitration provision in such an agreement. On this theory, the ultimate source of authority to bind parties to labor arbitration is the Labor Management Relations Act, rather than the Federal Arbitration Act.

THE FUNCTION OF LABOR ARBITRATION

One distinguishing feature of a collective bargaining relationship is that the parties (employer and union) are generally bound to deal with each other over an extended period. In most instances, moreover, any dispute regarding a working condition will have implications beyond the individual dispute. That is, whatever rule is adopted to resolve one dispute regarding one employee may become the rule for all, or a large portion of, the employees represented by the union.

At the same time, the possibility that every individual dispute could produce a strike or other disruption is too grave a risk to be ignored. A mechanism is required to resolve disputes, against the backdrop of the continuing relationship of the parties, but with the understanding that a swift, reasonably informed answer is preferable to the labor unrest that could result if every dispute could provoke a strike, or if every dispute could be tied up in litigation for years.

Arbitration is a neat solution to this problem. A professional corps of arbitrators, generally very experienced in labor law issues, helps to establish and apply a system of justice that both union and employer can accept over the course of a relationship that may span many years. Where a collective bargaining agreement may have left out the details on how to deal with some conditions of employment, moreover, the arbitration process may fill in the gaps in the collective bargaining agreement. In effect, arbitrators serve much of the law-making function that government administrative agencies can serve by applying and interpreting the general directions of the legislature. In the collective bargaining context, the arbitrator applies and interprets the general directions of the employer and the union, as reflected in their agreement.

THE LABOR ARBITRATION PROCESS

The union plays a key role in the labor arbitration process. The union represents the grievant (generally an employee) and can apply its considerable resources (and counsel) to the advancement of the grievant's claim. The union, however, also "owns" the grievance, and has the ability to compromise claims, or advance positions, for the good of the membership as a whole, not just the individual grievant.

The conduct of a labor arbitration proceeding is generally similar to proceedings for commercial arbitration. Discovery is generally limited, and the emphasis is on a swift, abbreviated schedule for hearing and decision. The parties may adopt relatively detailed codes of procedure for their labor arbitration (set forth in the collective bargaining agreement itself) or may agree to use procedures set forth in the labor arbitration rules of an arbitration-sponsoring organization.

Because the Labor Management Relations Act, rather than the Federal Arbitration Act, is the principal source of legislative authority for labor arbitration, the review and enforcement of labor arbitration awards is not guided by the FAA standards and procedures. The Labor Management Relations Act provides very little guidance on how such review and enforcement should be conducted. As a result, the federal courts have adopted a common law for review of labor arbitration awards.

In general, courts recognize that, so long as a labor arbitrator's award "draws its essence from the collective bargaining agreement," the award will not be upset. Although an arbitrator may not ignore the plain language of a labor contract, an arbitrator's findings of fact and interpretation of the contract are entitled to substantial deference. Even if the court is convinced that the arbitrator has committed a factual or legal error, the award will be sustained, so long as it is at least arguably supported by the language of the collective bargaining agreement.

An award procured by outright dishonesty or fraud would, no doubt, be invalidated, but such would be the extremely rare case. Less rare, but still quite unusual, would be circumstances in which an arbitrator's award was clearly inconsistent with public policy. Courts often suggest that such limited exception to the enforcement of labor arbitration awards applies only where the public policy is explicit, well-defined and dominant.

The most prominent of the potential public policy exceptions involves federal and state anti-discrimination laws. Such laws are independent sources of rights, such that a collective bargaining agreement's provision for arbitration of disputes arguably does not compel arbitration of statutory claims. Even if arbitration of claimed violations of the discrimination laws may be compelled, moreover, an arbitration award in clear violation of the discrimination laws would arguably be invalid on public policy grounds. The law regarding the interaction between the labor statutes and the anti-discrimination statutes, however, is unstable and developing.

Employment Arbitration

SOURCES OF LAW

Unlike the collective bargaining relationships that develop between unions and employers, non-union employment relationships are not covered by the federal labor statutes. As a result, there has, at times, been some confusion on the sources of law for employment arbitration.

According to one view, the Federal Arbitration Act, which applies to any "contract evidencing a transaction involving interstate commerce," could be read to apply only to commercial contracts. Indeed, the FAA expressly excludes from its coverage "contracts of employment of seamen, railroad employees, or any other class of workers engaged in . . . interstate commerce." Until recently, there was at least some authority for the proposition that the FAA did not apply to any employment contract.

The Supreme Court decision in *Circuit City Stores, Inc. v. Adams,* 532 U.S. 105, 121 S.Ct. 1302, 149 L.Ed.2d 234 (2001), laid that issue to rest. The Court definitively held that the FAA's coverage is not limited to commercial contracts, and that the exemption for certain classes of transportation workers was not meant to exclude all employment contracts from the application of the Act. Under the *Circuit City* rule, an arbitration provision in an employment contract (so long as the contract is not purely intrastate in scope) is enforceable under the terms of the FAA. Indeed, because the FAA generally preempts inconsistent state legislation, a state probably could not enact a statute aimed at invalidating or restricting the enforceability of employment arbitration agreements.

THE EMPLOYMENT ARBITRATION PROCESS

Unlike labor arbitrations, where a union plays an important role, in an employment arbitration proceeding, by definition, there is no union. Instead, an employer and employee will generally have entered into an individual contract of employment, with a clause providing for arbitration in the event of disputes under the contract.

The procedures for employment arbitration can be highly variable. As with ordinary commercial contracts, the parties may either agree to specific arbitration procedures in their contract, or may agree to adopt the procedures of an arbitration-sponsoring organ- ization. In practice, the terms of the arbitration procedure will most likely be chosen by the employer, as it is rare for an employ- ee to have negotiating leverage and much experience with the arbitration process.

The combination of the absence of a union representative and the lack of employee bargaining over the arbitration process can mean that some employment arbitration clauses are distinctly one-sided, in favor of the employer. Courts in some instances have suggested that particularly egregious arbitration systems (e.g., systems where the arbitrator is chosen by the employer, or where the cost of the arbitration to the employee makes assertion of a claim prohibi- tively expensive) may be invalidated.

ARBITRATION OF STATUTORY RIGHTS

From an employer's perspective, the agreement to arbitrate claims by an employee may have several benefits. Not only is arbitration often cheaper and faster than ordinary civil litigation, the agree- ment to arbitrate may protect an employer from some of the great- est risks of civil litigation. There is no jury in arbitration, and the risk of a huge, unwarranted award is greatly reduced by the fact that most arbitrators are seasoned professionals, unlikely to be swayed by emotion or superficial argument. Discovery is limited in arbitration, which means that an employer will rarely face the burdensome fishing expeditions that can occur in ordinary litiga- tion. And, perhaps most importantly, class action litigation is unheard of in arbitration, which reduces incentives to plaintiffs' lawyers, and can avoid the danger of a large award based on an accumulation of claims.

With these advantages in mind, most employers have every incen- tive to make any employment arbitration clause as broad as possi- ble. Claimants and their counsel, in turn, have searched for ways to defeat such clauses after disputes arise, and to gain access to ordinary civil litigation processes for at least some of their claims. The principal battleground in this regard has centered on statutory rights (in particular, claims under the anti-discrimination laws).

The Supreme Court, in *Alexander v. Gardner-Denver Co.,* 415 U.S. 36, 94 S.Ct. 1011, 39 L.Ed.2d 147 (1974), held that a claim under Title VII of the Civil Rights Act of 1964 was not precluded by an arbitrator's decision that the claimant had been discharged by the employer for "just cause." The Court suggested that, because Title VII rights are granted by statute, not contract, an agreement to arbitrate disputes would not encompass such rights.

The *Gardner-Denver* decision, however, has been greatly limited in scope. In *Gilmer v. Interstate/Johnson Lane Corp.,* 500 U.S. 20, 111 S.Ct. 1647, 114 L.Ed.2d 26 (1991), the Supreme Court held that an employee could be compelled to arbitrate an age discrimination claim where he had generally agreed to arbitration of "any controversy" with his employer. The *Gilmer* Court distinguished *Gardner-Denver,* noting (among other things) that the dispute in *Gardner-Denver* arose out of a collective bargaining relationship, such that the union controlled the arbitration process. The Court concluded that there was a "tension between collective representation and individual statutory rights."

The divergence between *Gardner-Denver* and *Gilmer* thus appears to mean that individual statutory claims may not be precluded by an arbitration provision in a collective bargaining agreement, but may be precluded by a similar provision in a non-union employment contract. There are, however, subsequent decisions with differing results. Some decisions suggest that a collective bargaining agreement arbitration provision should preclude separate civil litigation of a statutory claim. Other decisions, by contrast, suggest that arbitration of individual statutory claims are not precluded by an arbitration agreement, even where that agreement arises out of a non-union employment relationship. The precise course of law in this area has yet to be charted.

Most recently, the Supreme Court's decision in *EEOC v. Waffle House, Inc.,* No. 99-1823, 2002 WL 4673 (S. Ct. Jan. 15, 2002), established that the EEOC was not barred from pursuing discrimination claims against an employer in court, despite the fact that the affected employee had signed a valid arbitration agreement. It remains to be seen whether this decision will be considered by employers as materially altering their incentives for using arbitration as a dispute resolution mechanism. Critics of the decision have suggested that the inability to concentrate dispute resolution in a single forum may make arbitration a less attractive alternative.

In light of the *Gilmer* decision, representatives from the AAA and other organizations interested in labor and employment dispute resolution established a Task Force on Alternative Dispute Resolution in Employment. In 1995, the Task Force issued a due process protocol for mediation and arbitration of statutory claims arising out of employment relationships.

The protocol does not address all possible issues in employment arbitration. The Task Force members, for example, could not agree on whether pre-dispute arbitration agreements were acceptable. The points of agreement among the Task Force members, moreover, are relatively modest (such as the requirement that arbitrators be neutral and well-trained).

The due process protocol, nevertheless, is a useful starting point for constructing an employment arbitration system. The AAA, in particular, reserves the right to refuse to administer an arbitration proceeding involving statutory claims where the arbitration system does not conform to the protocol. The AAA rules for arbitration of employment disputes, moreover, take account of the protocol.

Within these broad boundaries of due process, however, parties are generally free, in employment arbitration as in commercial arbitration, to adopt procedures that suit their individual needs. The major arbitration-sponsoring organizations (such as the AAA) offer specialized rules for employment arbitration proceedings, but parties are not required to use any particular arbitration-sponsoring organization, or set of rules, for employment arbitration. Despite the existence of the Task Force due process protocols, the precise requirements for due process in this area are still being developed largely on a case-by-case basis by individual arbitrators and reviewing courts.

REVIEW OF EMPLOYMENT ARBITRATION AWARDS

Because non-union employment arbitration proceedings are considered the equivalent of commercial arbitrations, the rules governing commercial arbitration govern review and enforcement of awards. Where the employment contract arguably affects interstate commerce, the FAA will apply, and will supply the rules for such review and enforcement. Where the contract is purely intrastate, equivalent state arbitration laws will apply.

These federal and state arbitration laws generally do not make distinctions between the procedures for review that might be applied to arbitration of different types of disputes. Thus, while one might argue that employment relationships deserve a more searching review of arbitration decisions by the courts, there is no general sense in the case law that different standards of review should be applied to employment (versus commercial) arbitration awards. In general, most courts are highly deferential to the decisions of arbitrators.

Consumer Arbitration

INCREASING POPULARITY

Just as arbitration can help an employer control its risks in disputes with its employees, arbitration can be of great advantage to manufacturers, distributors and other businesses that face the potential for burdensome, costly litigation arising out of disputes with the consumers to whom they sell. Arbitration, as previously noted, can help reduce the cost and time required for litigation, and may also control the risks that enormous jury verdicts and class actions can create in civil litigation.

In our increasingly global market for goods and services, moreover, businesses may face the prospect of multiple lawsuits, in multiple jurisdictions, whenever a sustained dispute with consumers arises. The choice of arbitration can reduce the cost and burden to the business by fixing a single set of procedures (and perhaps a single venue) for resolution of all such disputes. Indeed, with the increasing popularity of the Internet and electronic transactions, the use of arbitration may be a critical method to avoid nationwide, and even worldwide, litigation whenever a consumer problem arises.

LIMITS ON STANDARD FORMS

Consumer contracts are almost always standard form contracts. Although there may be a great deal of consumer choice (in terms of price, type of good or service, and even major contract terms like length of warranty), the standard form contract is almost always take-it-or-leave-it. The consumer and the business do not haggle over the provisions of a standard form contract. In many instances, the consumer may not even read the contract.

The fact that an arbitration clause may be included in a contract of "adhesion," a standard form where the parties do not bargain over terms, does not by itself make the arbitration clause unenforceable. To demonstrate that the arbitration clause is "unconscionable," i.e., so unfair that it should not be enforced, more is required. Although the law of contracts varies from state to state, generally an unconscionable contract involves some elements of unfairness in the bargaining process (standard form, lack of bargaining, and perhaps some indication that the significance of the term was hidden or not fully explained), coupled with some unfairness in the clause itself. Challenges to the fairness of arbitration clauses in consumer contracts have taken many forms, some of which are summarized below.

COSTS IN EXCESS OF THE VALUE OF THE CLAIM

One frequent challenge to consumer arbitration is that the fees for initiating an arbitration, plus the arbitrator's fees, may dwarf the value of the individual consumer's claim. As a result, the argument goes, consumers may be effectively denied any remedy for their claims.

Many arbitration-sponsoring organizations, however, have adopted special rules for no-cost or low-cost arbitration of consumer claims. In some instances, moreover, an institutional proponent of a standard form arbitration clause may agree, in advance, to pay the costs of arbitration.

The Supreme Court's decision in *Green Tree Financial Corp.– Alabama v. Randolph*, 531 U.S. 79, 121 S.Ct. 513, 148 L.Ed.2d 373 (2000), held that the mere assertion that excessive arbitration fees might deter exercise of consumer rights would not suffice to invalidate an arbitration clause. The Court held that the consumer bore the burden to show the excessive nature of the fees and that there were no alternatives for conducting the arbitration at low cost to the consumer.

INABILITY TO PURSUE CLASS ACTIONS

Related to the argument regarding prohibitive fees is the argument made in many instances by consumers and their counsel that the inability to pursue class actions in arbitration may effectively curtail the enforcement of consumer rights. The argument is that consumers with relatively small individual claims will not proceed unless their claims can be consolidated, such that the prospect of larger recoveries will justify the cost of proceeding.

Courts, with some exceptions, have not been very receptive to this argument. Because arbitration is a matter of contract, and because arbitration clauses typically do not permit class actions, consumers who agree to arbitration effectively waive their right to pursue class actions. Waiver of class action rights is otherwise permissible. So long as the costs of arbitration are not unduly prohibitive, waiver of class action rights by choice of arbitration may be effective.

ONE-SIDED ARBITRATION CLAUSES

Consumers have, in some instances, attempted to challenge arbitration clauses that bind consumers to arbitrate their claims against an institution such as a corporation, but that permit the institution to bring any of its own claims (such as for foreclosure or repossession) in court. These arguments have met with relatively little success. Parties are not required to agree to arbitrate all their claims. An institution may thus reasonably insist that arbitration is efficient for certain kinds of claims, but not for others.

More likely to succeed is the argument that an arbitration clause is one-sided because the method for selecting arbitrators favors the institution over the consumer. The broad principle that "no man can be his own judge" would most likely prohibit an institution from choosing one of its own operatives as arbitrator for any claims against the institution. Where the institution entirely controls the arbitration selection process (even if the arbitrator is arguably independent of the parties), moreover, a challenge for one-sidedness may be successful.

ARBITRATION OF STATUTORY CLAIMS

As with arbitration of other types of disputes, the trend in consumer arbitration is to recognize that statutory claims may properly be the subject of an arbitration agreement. Thus, where parties agree to arbitrate all claims arising out of a consumer contract, courts generally hold that a consumer's statutory claims are encompassed within that agreement.

Where the nature of the arbitration process may hinder the effective enforcement of statutory rights, however, courts may be less willing to enforce an agreement to arbitrate as the exclusive remedy for the consumer. Thus, the combination of a statutory claim plus one or more of the indicia of unconscionability summarized above may be the basis for invalidating an arbitration agreement.

The invalidation of an arbitration agreement, as written, does not, however, necessarily mean that the consumer will be free to pursue all claims in court. Courts in some instances have strained to reform an arbitration clause, to permit the enforcement of the essential bargain for arbitration, but with offending provisions (excessive fees, one-sided arbitrator selection, etc.) omitted or otherwise ameliorated.

DUE PROCESS PROTOCOLS FOR CONSUMER ARBITRATION

In response to the collision between the increasing popularity of consumer arbitration and the increasing judicial scrutiny of the fairness of consumer arbitration procedures, several arbitration sponsoring organizations (the American Arbitration Association and JAMS/Endispute, among others) have adopted minimum due process protocols for consumer arbitration. These due process protocols aim to set standards for arbitration of consumer disputes. Where an arbitration clause calls for arbitration administered by an organization with such a due process protocol, the arbitration-sponsoring organization may refuse to administer the arbitration unless these minimum due process standards are met.

These due process protocols vary in their terms and in their specificity. In general, however, the aim of such protocols is to provide fair, balanced and affordable arbitration procedures for consumers. The requirement of a low-cost method of initiating and conducting an arbitration, for example, is embodied in such protocols. Similarly, such protocols typically seek to ensure that the selection of an arbitrator is a fair process, with input from both sides. These minimum due process protocols may affect the conduct of consumer arbitration more indirectly by helping to establish a consensus on the minimum due process standards for arbitration. For institutional litigants, such as corporations, there may be some enhanced certainty that an arbitration program will be enforceable if it can be favorably evaluated under one of the due process protocols.

Despite these due process protocols, however, the controversy over consumer arbitration is likely to persist. Institutions generally have powerful incentives to favor arbitration (lower cost, lower risk and greater certainty being the principal benefits). Consumers and their lawyers, by contrast, often have powerful incentives to favor litigation in court after a dispute arises, including access to the class action device, right to jury trial, and broader discovery of institutional documents and witnesses. The inherent conflict between these interests virtually guarantees that challenges to consumer arbitration will continue for many years.

Securities Arbitration

Arbitration in the securities industry differs from commercial, labor and consumer arbitration in many ways, some of which are outlined below. Indeed, practitioners in this area effectively form a unique group, with a cohesive body of collective experience that differs from the often variable experience in other forms of arbitration.

ROLE OF THE SELF-REGULATORY ORGANIZATIONS

The securities industry in the United States is largely controlled by self-regulatory organizations ("SROs"). These SROs (chiefly the

New York Stock Exchange and the National Association of Securities Dealers) adopt rules and regulations for their member broker-dealers. The rules of the SROs, in turn, are reviewed by the Securities and Exchange Commission. The result is a uniformity of professional standards that is rare in other industries.

Arbitration in the securities industry is greatly affected by the influence of the SROs. The NYSE and the NASD both offer arbitration administration services, and the vast majority of securities industry arbitrations are administered under these programs. (The American Arbitration Association, which has adopted specific arbitration rules for the securities industry, administers most of the relatively small remainder of securities industry arbitrations.) The result of widespread administration by the SROs (backed, ultimately, by SEC review of procedures) is a much more uniform process for arbitration in the securities industry than in most other industries.

The SROs, moreover, administer thousands of cases each year. Arbitrators and practitioners in the securities industry thus can gain very substantial experience with arbitration practices, contributing to the common understanding, and enhanced uniformity, of procedures.

MINIMUM STANDARDS FOR SECURITIES INDUSTRY ARBITRATION

The SROs have adopted a number of rules that are designed to improve the fairness and effectiveness of securities industry arbitration, from the customer's viewpoint. These rules include:

 ♦ ***Arbitration at the choice of the customer:*** Although the broker-dealer is not required to have an arbitration clause in its contract with a customer, SRO rules generally provide that a customer may elect to pursue SRO-sponsored arbitration, at his choice. This rule reverses the circumstance in some consumer contracts, where the consumer is forced to arbitrate his claims, but the institution is not required to arbitrate its own claims.

♦ ***Lower up-front fees:*** The SROs generally provide that a customer need pay only a relatively modest fee to initiate an arbitration proceeding.

♦ ***Automatic service of pleadings:*** The SRO rules generally provide that initiation of a customer claim requires only filing of pleadings with the SRO. The SRO will serve the pleading on the respondent broker-dealer.

♦ ***Location of arbitration hearing:*** An SRO arbitration administrator will almost always set the location for arbitration hearings to suit the convenience of the customer.

♦ ***Disciplinary referrals and publication of awards:*** Unlike most other arbitration proceedings, which are treated as confidential, securities industry arbitrations are recognized as infused with a public character. Thus, if an arbitrator believes that a broker has engaged in wrongful conduct, he will refer the broker to the SRO's disciplinary administration. The results of securities industry arbitrations, moreover, are generally open to the public. Public exposure of wrongful conduct is thus more of a risk in securities arbitration than in other areas.

♦ ***Automatic enforcement of awards:*** Unlike parties in other arbitration proceedings, where an award is not self-enforcing, a prevailing customer in a securities industry arbitration may rely on SRO rules that require broker-dealers to pay any arbitration award promptly or face disciplinary action. Thus, a customer may not need to follow the relatively cumbersome process of obtaining an award and later initiating a court proceeding to confirm the award.

ARBITRATION OF SECURITIES INDUSTRY EMPLOYMENT DISPUTES

In addition to customer claims, the SROs also handle most employment claims of registered representatives against their employer broker-dealers. As with sponsored arbitration of customer claims, the procedures for arbitration of securities industry employment claims are more uniform, and often more favorable to the individual, than arbitration in other industries, where the procedures are generally chosen by large institutions.

ETHICS AND PROFESSIONAL RESPONSIBILITY IN ARBITRATION

The sources and terms of any standards of ethics and professional responsibility applicable to arbitration are often poorly defined, unlike the well-established and well-understood codes of ethics and professional responsibility relating to practice before judicial bodies. As a result, practitioners and arbitrators often must deal with a variety of ethical and professional responsibility questions, many of which have no definitive answer.

Sources of Rules

The sources of rules potentially applicable in an arbitration proceeding are many. The arbitration agreement itself may state some basic rules regarding the conduct of the proceeding. If the parties have chosen an arbitration-sponsoring organization, moreover, the rules of the organization will generally provide more detail regarding the conduct of the arbitration. Such provisions in agreements and arbitration organization rules, however, rarely address the full range of ethical and professional responsibility issues that may arise in arbitration.

So too, the FAA and parallel state statutes generally establish procedures for the review of arbitration awards. Review of an award may, to some degree, involve review of ethical and professional responsibility issues that may have arisen during the arbitration. Yet, the purpose of the FAA and state statutes is not to establish uniform rules for ethics and professional responsibility in arbitration. At best, judicial review of arbitration awards offers only sporadic insight into such issues.

There have been several attempts to establish uniform codes of ethics and professional responsibility in arbitration. Most significantly, in 1977 the American Bar Association and the American Arbitration Association jointly developed the Code of Ethics for Arbitrators in Commercial Disputes. This Code was the product of extensive basic research and public comments. The Code addresses a host of potential problems, including bias, breaches of confidentiality, delay and procedural fairness.

Similar codes have been established by other organizations, in other areas. In 1951, the National Academy of Arbitrators, the AAA and the Federal Mediation and Conciliation Service established the Code of Responsibility for Arbitrators of Labor-Management Disputes, which was revised in 1975. In 1987, the International Bar Association published a set of guidelines called Ethics for International Arbitrators. The Society of Maritime Arbitrators has published a Code of Ethics as well.

These codes, while helpful, are not a panacea. At best, they are binding only in certain industries and in arbitrations sponsored by certain organizations. The codes, moreover, tend to focus on the ethical obligations of arbitrators, rather than the behavior of advocates appearing before arbitration tribunals. Despite these limitations, the codes are valuable attempts to recognize and address the important ethical and professional responsibility issues that may arise in the course of arbitration. Several of the most important issues are discussed below.

Unauthorized Practice of Law

Arbitration proceedings may take place in a variety of locations, depending upon the choices of the parties, the rules of the sponsoring organization, and the directions of the arbitrators and the staff of the sponsoring organization. Often, attorneys admitted in one jurisdiction will find themselves being asked to represent a client in an arbitration proceeding that takes place in a jurisdiction where they are not admitted to practice law. The question, in those circumstances, is whether representing the client in arbitration proceedings taking place in a location outside the jurisdiction where the attorney is admitted constitutes the unauthorized practice of law in that other jurisdiction.

The majority rule in the United States appears to permit representation of a client in an arbitration proceeding that takes place outside the jurisdiction where an attorney is licensed to practice law. This rule appears to take account of the practical realities of arbitration. If attorneys were required to obtain permission (from local bar authorities or local courts) before proceeding with representations in arbitration, the speed and efficiency of arbitration could be impeded. Indeed, parties might be more likely to insist on arbitration in only a few major commercial centers, where counsel experienced in arbitration are most readily available.

Despite this majority rule favoring flexible representation in arbitration, there are some significant exceptions. In *Birbower, Montalbano Gordon & Frank, P.C. v. Superior Court,* 949 P.2d 1 (Cal. Sup. Ct. 1998), the California Supreme Court held that a New York law firm violated a California statute prohibiting the unauthorized practice of law, by using counsel who were not admitted in California to initiate arbitration proceedings in California and to negotiate a settlement on behalf of a California client in California. As a result, the court held, the firm could not recover fees for services performed in California.

In response to the *Birbower* decision, the California legislature amended the unauthorized practice of law statute (at least temporarily) to provide an exception for participation in private domestic arbitration proceedings. (Such a statutory exception already existed for international arbitrations.) Under the new law, an attorney admitted to the bar of another state may represent a party in an arbitration proceeding in California, so long as the attorney files a certificate setting forth his professional information, confirming that he is not engaged in substantial business in California, and subjecting himself to the jurisdiction of California courts with respect to disciplinary matters. Additionally, the out-of-state attorney must name local counsel, who will serve as the attorney of record.

The *Birbower* decision and its aftermath illustrate the uncertain status of out-of-state attorneys. Counsel appearing in an arbitration proceeding in a location outside the jurisdiction where they are authorized to practice law are well-advised to check local rules and court decisions regarding the unauthorized practice of law, and to consult with the staff of the arbitration-sponsoring institution (if any) for their experience in the specific jurisdiction.

Counsel should be particularly circumspect whenever representation in an arbitration proceeding requires appearance in court in a jurisdiction where they are not licensed for purposes of some ancillary proceeding related to the arbitration. Even where counsel appear on behalf of a responding party (such that they have not themselves invoked the power of the court), appearance in court without license or *pro hac vice* admission almost always risks a charge of unauthorized practice of law.

The law in jurisdictions outside the United States is even more fluid and variable. Although it is quite normal for practitioners from different countries to appear as counsel and arbitrators in an international arbitration, many such arbitration proceedings take place in a few major commercial centers, where the law on arbitration practice and procedure is well-established and stable. Before embarking on representation of a party in an arbitration proceeding in a more obscure location, consultation with local counsel may be essential.

Unethical and Unprofessional Behavior During the Course of Arbitration

The vast majority of unethical and unprofessional behavior that may take place during the course of arbitration proceedings can be controlled by an arbitrator's use of the considerable discretionary power the arbitrator ordinarily enjoys in arbitration proceedings. A party or lawyer who engages in dilatory tactics, who advances frivolous arguments, or who refuses to cooperate in the information gathering process, for example, may be subjected to a variety of explicit or unstated sanctions. The arbitrator may draw adverse inferences, adjust schedules, impose costs, or otherwise take steps to ensure the fairness of the proceedings.

Arbitrators, however, have been reluctant to regulate in certain areas of ethics and professional responsibility. For example, where a party claims that counsel for another party is laboring under a conflict of interest, arbitrators often have not intervened. The right to counsel of one's choice is a basic right and implicates public policy issues that arbitrators often do not wish to address. Disqualification of counsel, moreover, may place any award ultimately rendered at risk of being vacated.

Similarly, in court proceedings, where counsel for a party appears to have direct personal knowledge regarding the merits of the dispute, the attorney might be disqualified as a lawyer-witness. In arbitration, again, arbitrators are often reluctant to interfere with the attorney-client relationship.

Resort to the courts to address such issues during the course of arbitration proceedings, moreover, is unlikely to succeed. In general, aside from determining whether a valid arbitration agreement exists, and whether it covers the dispute at issue, the FAA and parallel state statutes do not contemplate court intervention before an arbitration proceeding is completed. At the completion of the arbitration, moreover, the focus is generally on the validity of the award, rather than on the conduct of counsel during the course of the proceeding.

Ethical Standards for Arbitrator Behavior

As previously noted, the ABA/AAA Code of Ethics for Arbitrators in Commercial Disputes sets forth rather comprehensive guidelines for arbitrators, which are generally reflected in the ethics rules of several other organizations. Many of these guidelines address the essential qualifications of an arbitrator. An arbitrator, for example, should ensure that he has the essential competence, and time, to conduct an arbitration. An arbitrator should also charge a reasonable fee for his services, and should maintain adequate records to support his time and expense charges.

An arbitrator, moreover, should generally be independent and unbiased. Arbitrators are often compared in this regard to judges, who must meet relatively strict standards to avoid the appearance of impropriety. Yet, it must be recognized that arbitrators are often chosen for their expertise in a particular field. Such expertise is generally gained as a result of wide experience in the field. Arbitrators, moreover, are often busy professionals, with ongoing business, social and personal relationships. It has been suggested, therefore, that while judges must avoid any appearance of interest in or bias regarding a matter, an arbitrator's award can be upset only where there is a direct, definite interest or bias that can be demonstrated with certainty. The FAA standard for vacating an award (for "corruption, fraud or other undue means") suggests that an award will not routinely be upset on ordinary claims of partiality or bias.

Despite this perhaps relaxed standard of impartiality, the rules of most arbitration-sponsoring organizations require disclosure of most professional, financial, social and personal relationships between an arbitrator and the parties or their counsel. Deliberate failure to disclose such a relationship, moreover, may itself be considered unethical conduct, even though the relationship alone might not necessarily be a sufficient ground to vacate an award.

Similarly, although it is often useful to compare the investigation and hearing processes of arbitration to the pre-trial and trial processes in a court, there is generally no requirement that an arbitration mirror all judicial procedures. Thus, while ethics codes and the rules of most arbitration-sponsoring organizations require that arbitrators allow each party a fair opportunity to present its case, the precise procedure is generally within the discretion of the arbitrator. The FAA and parallel state statutes generally will not permit a court to vacate an award unless the denial of an opportunity to make a presentation constitutes an abuse of that discretion.

The arbitrator's ethical duty to reach an independent, impartial decision generally operates within the confines of that discretion. Thus, it would certainly be improper for an arbitrator to announce that he will allow a presentation by one side only, or to indicate that he has decided the matter after hearing from only one side. Yet, short of such absolute pronouncements, it may often be difficult to determine that an arbitrator's rulings are the product of partiality or bias. The arbitrator's discretion to control the conduct of proceedings and the standard for judicial review of an arbitration award (where even clear error of law or fact may not suffice to upset the award) reduce successful challenges for bias or partiality to a minimum.

More likely to succeed are challenges based on *ex parte* communications with an arbitrator. Independent, neutral arbitrators should not engage parties in *ex parte* dialogue, except as necessary to schedule proceedings and to deal with other routine administrative matters. The rules of most arbitration-sponsoring organizations, and most ethics codes, forbid such contact, on the theory that a party cannot confront the other party's factual submissions and arguments when it is not present, and the process of arbitration may be tainted when only one side is heard.

Except with the consent of the parties, moreover, an arbitrator should not engage in mediation or other attempts to devise a settlement of the dispute. An arbitrator may, however, offer assistance in mediating the dispute, or otherwise encourage the parties to seek a consensual resolution of their dispute.

Despite the rules forbidding *ex parte* communications, ethics codes and the rules of most arbitration-sponsoring organizations allow an arbitrator to proceed with only one party present, so long as it is clear that the other party has received proper notice of the proceeding. Thus, for example, the rules of most sponsoring organizations permit an arbitrator to enter a default award where the moving party demonstrates the basis for the award and the other parties fail to appear or respond after proper notice has been given.

Generally, in conducting arbitration proceedings, an arbitrator's principal obligation is to provide a fair process for resolution of the dispute, in accordance with the agreement of the parties and the rules (if any) of the chosen arbitration-sponsoring organization. The arbitrator should strive to maintain the dignity and decorum of the process, recognizing the importance and seriousness of the issues to the disputants. An arbitrator may take an active role in the information-gathering process, asking questions, calling for witnesses and documents, or otherwise shaping the process to ensure that justice is done.

An arbitrator should take steps to ensure that an arbitration proceeding is concluded swiftly and efficiently, where possible. An arbitrator should make all reasonable efforts to prevent delaying tactics, harassment or abuse of a party, and any other disruption or misuse of the arbitration process.

An arbitrator is obligated to render a clear, concise award. An arbitrator should decide the case on the merits and not simply "cut the baby in half." Nor should an arbitrator allow his personal feelings to affect the outcome of the case. An arbitrator should decide only the issues that have been presented by the parties. An arbitrator may not delegate the obligation to decide the case to anyone (although, in certain cases, an arbitrator may arrange for the appointment of one or more experts to assist the arbitrator in understanding the issues in the case).

Once the award is rendered, the arbitrator generally should not involve himself in the process of moving to enforce the award. Nor should a dissenting arbitrator in a three-arbitrator tribunal involve himself in any motion to vacate the award. An arbitrator, moreover, should avoid involvement with the parties after the arbitration is concluded, for a reasonable period, in circumstances that might reasonably create an appearance that the arbitrator had been influenced by the expectation that the relationship would develop.

Special Role of Party-Appointed Arbitrators

In some cases, parties agree to a system of arbitrator selection in which each party is permitted to select one arbitrator. Typically, the two party-appointed arbitrators then choose the third, "neutral" arbitrator. This system is often used in large, international commercial cases.

The rules of most arbitration-sponsoring organizations relax the standards for behavior by an arbitrator appointed by one of the parties. A party-appointed arbitrator generally may have a preexisting relationship with the party who appoints him and may even be predisposed to vote in favor of that party. A party-appointed arbitrator, moreover, generally is permitted to have certain *ex parte* discussions with the party who appoints him. For example, a party-appointed arbitrator may generally consult with the party who appoints him when such consultation is necessary in the process of choosing the third, neutral arbitrator for the proceeding.

These somewhat relaxed standards for arbitrator behavior, however, may have their limits. Even a party-appointed arbitrator, for example, could not accept extraordinary payment in exchange for a favorable vote in a case. Such behavior would almost certainly qualify as "corruption" of the arbitration process. The agreement of the parties and the rules of some arbitration-sponsoring organizations also may provide that even a party-appointed arbitrator must remain strictly "neutral." In many instances, moreover, even if the party-appointed arbitrator may be less than neutral, any limitations on the arbitrator's independence and neutrality must generally be disclosed.

Ethical Issues in International Arbitration

Particularly problematic for most American lawyers and arbitrators are the ethical issues that may arise in the course of international arbitration proceedings. In many such proceedings, a significant issue is the choice of law applicable to the conduct of the proceedings. This choice of law may have a great deal to do with the ethical obligations of counsel and arbitrators.

For example, in most European countries, the attorney-client privilege is a relatively narrow right. Communications between corporate officers and their in-house counsel may not be considered privileged in such countries. Other restrictions on the privilege also may apply (such as the fact that the privilege belongs to the lawyer, not the client, in most European systems). American practitioners may be forced to deal with these more restrictive privilege rules where the arbitration agreement calls for application of European law, where the arbitration-sponsoring organization is European, where an arbitration is conducted in a European country or where one or more of the arbitrators come from a European country. Thus, what might be considered malpractice in the United States (such as failure to guard attorney-client privileged communications) may be acceptable (or even mandatory) in an international arbitration. Further, where the privilege is limited, an American lawyer may need to be more circumspect about communications with a client; where the lawyer might otherwise view himself as having an obligation to report regularly to a client on developments, the limits of the privilege may mean that such reports cannot be as complete.

Similarly, in most European systems, attorneys may view themselves more as officers of the court than as advocates. In such systems, an attorney may view himself as having an obligation to correct errors in the process, even when they work to a client's advantage. Thus, in dealing with European co-counsel, American lawyers may grapple with competing views of their roles.

Added to the ethical burden in dealing with foreign legal systems is the necessity, in many instances, of having local counsel for purposes of an international arbitration proceeding. In some instances, conducting an arbitration proceeding in another country may be viewed as the unauthorized practice of law. In most cases, moreover, an American lawyer cannot properly claim competence in dealing with foreign law issues. As a result, it is often necessary to engage foreign counsel. Where the American lawyer deals with foreign counsel, it is often important to clarify roles and relationships. To avoid charges of fee-splitting, for example, it may be preferable to have the client, rather than the American lawyer, engage the foreign counsel. Similarly, it may be desirable to make clear to the client that supervision of the foreign counsel on foreign law issues is not within the American lawyer's ken.

Despite these ethical conundrums, it is a common occurrence for American lawyers to become involved in international arbitration proceedings. In most cases, such proceedings represent a useful middle ground for dispute resolution, blending portions of the legal culture and traditions of two or more nations. The struggle to maintain ethics and professional behavior in this blended environment may produce novel, and challenging, issues.

Confidentiality Restrictions

Privacy is often one of the principal factors that cause parties to choose arbitration for dispute resolution, rather than ordinary litigation. The rules of most arbitration-sponsoring organizations generally require that arbitration proceedings, and the results of arbitration proceedings, be kept confidential.

The obligation to maintain confidentiality may be problematic in some instances. For example, attorneys generally are required to report unprofessional behavior by other attorneys. Such reports must be made to bar associations, disciplinary committees and other regulators of professional conduct. Under ethical rules in some states, however, attorneys and arbitrators who observe unprofessional behavior in arbitration proceedings may be excused from their reporting obligations by virtue of their confidentiality duties in arbitration.

More generally, the obligation of confidentiality in arbitration means that lawyers and arbitrators should not reveal the details of confidential arbitration proceedings for purposes unrelated to the arbitration. It would, for example, almost certainly be unethical to profit from "inside" information gained in the course of a confidential arbitration proceeding, or to use such information to gain a competitive advantage over one of the parties. Revelation of the details of an arbitration proceeding for purposes of advertising professional services may also be prohibited. Summarizing a case without revealing details, for purposes of education or professional training, may be permissible.

The contours of these confidentiality rules depend, to a large degree, on the terms of the arbitration agreement and the rules (if any) of the applicable arbitration-sponsoring organization. Because the case law and volume of ethical opinions are relatively thin in this area, and because the issues are often quite case-specific, caution must be the basic rule before any revelation of confidential arbitration proceedings occurs.

ADR TERMS

Glossary of ADR Terms

Although this book generally concerns issues in arbitration, it is appropriate to set that specific form of alternative dispute resolution in the context of the wide variety of other alternative dispute resolution techniques that have become available in recent years. Alternative dispute resolution in general, and arbitration in particular, employ an array of terms to describe these procedures. This glossary of terms aims at introducing the reader to some of the many terms used in connection with alternative dispute resolution techniques.

Adjudication ❖ Adjudication includes any form of dispute resolution in which parties to the dispute present proof and arguments to a neutral third party who has the power to deliver a binding decision, generally based on objective standards. The term includes both arbitration and litigation.

Administrator ❖ Most ADR-sponsoring organizations provide for administration of matters unrelated to substantive dispute resolution (such as the choice of arbitrators and mediators, payment of fees, and many other issues) through a professional staff of administrators.

Alternative Dispute Resolution (ADR) ❖ ADR refers to a wide array of techniques that can be used to resolve disputes without formal adjudication through judge and jury. ADR processes usually involve the participation of independent parties, known as "neutrals." In some forms of ADR, neutrals issue decisions. In other forms, neutrals help parties resolve their own disputes. ADR includes arbitration, conciliation, mediation, negotiation and many other techniques. The objective of ADR generally is to offer a flexible, efficient and speedy way for people to resolve a dispute.

Appellate ADR ❖ Appellate ADR programs generally offer some form of mediation or conciliation, after decision by a judge or jury, and prior to consideration of the appeal by a panel of appeals court judges. In most programs, staff attorneys or outside lawyers conduct mandatory, pre-argument conferences in all cases, or in those cases that seem most likely to settle. Some appellate ADR programs are geared exclusively toward settlement, while other programs also address case management and procedural issues.

Arbitration ❖ Arbitration is the most traditional form of private dispute resolution. Arbitration involves submission of a dispute to a neutral or panel of neutrals for a decision to be rendered after hearing arguments and reviewing evidence. Arbitration can be "administered" (managed) by a variety of private organizations, or "non-administered" and managed solely by the parties and the arbitrator. It can be entered into by agreement at the time of the dispute, or chosen in pre-dispute clauses contained in the parties' underlying contract. Arbitration proceedings are generally less rigidly structured than formal court proceedings, and often can be concluded more quickly, with less cost. Depending on the situation, an arbitrator's decision can be either binding or non-binding. The exact nature and scope of the arbitration process is usually prescribed by contract, or otherwise agreed to between the parties.

Assessment ❖ Assessment involves an impartial analysis of a conflict situation, which is conducted by a neutral with an eye toward determining potential paths by which parties may reach a resolution of their conflict. The assessment process usually includes personally interviewing the parties, researching the history of the conflict, and attempting to find agreement as to the core issues around which the conflict has evolved. An assessment generally leads to the design of a means by which the parties may work with each other directly to resolve their dispute, an agreement on a further procedure for resolution of the dispute with the assistance of a neutral, or a decision that the conflict cannot be dealt with appropriately by ADR techniques.

Award ❖ An award is a decision of an arbitrator. Awards are made in writing and are enforceable in court under the Federal Arbitration Act and similar state statutes.

"Baseball" or "Final-Offer" Arbitration ❖ In baseball or final-offer arbitration, each party submits a proposed monetary award to the arbitrator. At the conclusion of the hearing, the arbitrator must choose one award amount, without modification. This approach imposes limits on the arbitrator's discretion and gives each party an incentive to offer a reasonable proposal, in the hope that the proposal will be accepted by the decision-maker. A related technique, referred to as "night baseball" arbitration, requires the arbitrator to make a decision without the benefit of the parties' proposals and then to make the award to the party whose proposal is closest to the amount that the arbitrator would have awarded.

Binding ❖ A legally enforceable decision or agreement resulting from a dispute resolution process is referred to as "binding" on the parties. Unless there has been fraud or some other defect in the arbitration procedure, a binding arbitration award is typically enforceable by a court with only limited grounds for review.

Bounded Arbitration ❖ In bounded arbitration, the parties agree privately without informing the arbitrator that the arbitrator's final award will be adjusted to conform to a bounded range. For example, if the claimant wants $250,000 and the respondent is willing to pay $50,000, their high-low bounded award agreement would provide that if the award is below $50,000, Respondent will pay at least $50,000; if the award exceeds $250,000, the payment will be reduced to $250,000. If the award is within that range, the parties will be bound by the figure in the arbitrator's award.

Case Valuation ❖ The case valuation process provides litigants in trial-ready cases with a written, non-binding assessment of the case's likely value, delivered by a neutral after a very short hearing. If the neutral's valuation is accepted by all parties, the case is settled for that amount. If any party rejects the neutral's assessment, the case proceeds to trial.

Caucus ❖ A caucus is a private meeting between a neutral (generally a mediator) and any one party, in which the neutral explores ways of resolving the dispute.

Claimant ❖ A claimant, also known as a plaintiff, is a party who files a claim in arbitration.

Co-mediation ❖ Co-mediation is a process in which there are two mediators who simultaneously or jointly conduct the process. Co-mediation is used in cases in which mediators with different areas of expertise would be useful, and for other purposes when more than one neutral would be appropriate.

Conciliation ❖ Conciliation is an informal process in which a neutral third party is positioned between the parties to create a channel for communications, usually by conveying messages between parties where it is preferable that they not meet face-to-face. A conciliator may also identify common ground and help re-establish direct communications between the parties. Conciliation sometimes leads to settlement. In some variations on the conciliation technique, the conciliator may be required to make a "recommendation" as to how the dispute should be settled if agreement cannot be reached by the parties during the process. Conciliation is often used in equal employment, domestic relations and public employee collective bargaining disputes.

Confidentiality ❖ Confidentiality is an important component of most ADR processes. Information shared during the course of a dispute resolution process is generally deemed private and is not to be revealed to anyone outside of the process. Typically, party expectations and legal requirements regarding confidentiality are discussed before an ADR process begins.

Confidential Listener ❖ In the confidential listener process, parties submit their settlement positions to a neutral, who (without relaying one side's confidential offer to the other) informs them whether their positions are within a negotiable range. The parties may agree that if the proposed figures are within a specified range of each other (for example, 15 percent), the parties may direct the neutral to so inform them and help them negotiate to narrow the gap. If the figures are not within the set range, the parties may repeat the process, or follow another ADR process.

Conflict ❖ Conflict is a broad term regarding any interaction between people with interests that are perceived as incompatible. Conflicts involving defined parties are often referred to as disputes.

Conflict Management ❖ Conflict management involves a philosophy and set of skills designed to assist people in better understanding and dealing with conflict as it arises in all aspects of their lives.

Consensus Building ❖ Consensus building is a method of seeking to resolve a multiple-party conflict, relying upon equal participation of all parties. The goal is generally to develop an agreement that all of the participants endorse.

Counterclaims ❖ In arbitration, counterclaims are counter-demands made by a respondent against a claimant. Counterclaims are not mere answers or denials of the claimant's allegations.

Court-Annexed ADR ❖ Court-annexed ADR programs are those that are operated, funded and/or sponsored by a court. In some instances, parties may be required or advised by the court to participate in such programs. In other instances, the ADR program is merely offered by the court.

Court-Annexed Arbitration ❖ In court-annexed arbitration, one or more arbitrators issue a non-binding judgment on the merits, after an expedited, adversarial hearing. In some programs, unless one of the parties rejects the non-binding ruling within a certain time period and asks to proceed to trial, the arbitration decision becomes final. In other programs, the arbitration decision remains non-binding without any need for a party to object, and simply serves as a guide for the parties to aid them in efforts to settle the case. Court-annexed arbitration is often used in small tort and contract cases, when litigation costs may be disproportionate to the amounts at stake.

Demand for Arbitration ❖ A demand for arbitration is a unilateral filing of a claim, which begins the arbitration process.

Dispute Review Board ❖ A dispute review board is a panel set up to adjudicate, mediate or settle claims on an ongoing basis. Dispute review boards are often established where parties have continuing relationships (as in construction projects) with repeated occasions for disputes to arise.

Early Neutral Evaluation (ENE) ❖ ENE is a court-annexed process in which parties and their counsel present the essential factual and legal bases of their positions to a neutral. The neutral gives the parties a non-binding prediction of the outcome, which may be useful in settlement discussions. Because the neutral offers an objective opinion, parties may be inclined to accept the advice. ENE can help parties and their counsel to determine the strengths and weaknesses of their case. ENE is generally used prior to significant discovery. If parties do not settle, ENE can serve as a case management technique by helping the parties to focus on the specific discovery they need to resolve the case.

Facilitator ❖ A facilitator is a neutral trained in the use of dispute resolution techniques who provides services to parties involved in a conflict. The facilitator provides procedural assistance to the parties, enhancing information exchange and working with the parties to develop and evaluate possible agreements that could lead to a resolution. Facilitation is also used to help parties reach a goal or complete a task to the mutual satisfaction of participants. Facilitation is often used when there are many interested parties or stakeholders, as distinguished from mediation, which tends to focus on a single-issue dispute between two parties.

Fact-Finding ❖ In a fact-finding process, the neutral fact-finder investigates a case either formally or informally, and issues a report. The fact-finder's report may include recommendations. The report may be used as the basis for settlement, and in some instances may be used to assist the judge or jury in the event of trial. Often, as a part of the fact-finding process, parties present arguments and evidence to the neutral. The neutral fact-finder, however, generally is not confined to evidence and argument from the parties, but may gather information through his/her own processes.

Grievance Procedures ❖ A grievance procedure is a dispute resolution process that may be offered by a public or private body. Employees, clients or members of the public are obliged to follow the grievance procedure to redress their complaints or grievances. Many grievance procedures provide for a multi-step dispute resolution process.

Hearing ❖ A hearing is a proceeding in which evidence is taken for the purpose of determining the facts of a dispute and reaching a decision based on that evidence.

Incentive Arbitration ❖ In incentive arbitration, parties agree to a penalty if one of them rejects the arbitrator's decision, resorts to litigation, and/or fails to improve his/her position by some specified percentage or formula. Penalties may include payment of attorneys' fees incurred in the litigation.

Mediation ❖ Mediation is a structured dispute resolution process in which a neutral assists parties to reach a negotiated settlement of their differences. The mediator uses a variety of skills and techniques to help parties communicate, negotiate, and reach agreements. While mediators may, under certain circumstances, make suggestions about potential resolutions to the parties, they generally have no authority to render binding decisions. The mediation process may involve a formal meeting or a series of meetings with the mediator "shuttling" between the parties, or an informal series of conversations assisted by the mediator. Mediation is confidential, and the information exchanged during the process is regarded as "without prejudice" communication for the purpose of settlement negotiations. The mediation process may involve counsel, but open communications between the parties as well as between their counsel is generally encouraged. Parties may engage in mediation as a result of a contract provision, by private agreement made when disputes arise, or as part of a court-annexed program that diverts cases to mediation. The mediation process is sometimes indiscriminately referred to as "facilitation" or "conciliation"; those terms, however, have their own separate meanings.

Mediation-Arbitration (Med-Arb) ❖ Mediation-arbitration employs a neutral selected to serve as both mediator and arbitrator in a dispute. It combines the voluntary techniques of persuasion, as in mediation, with an arbitrator's authority to issue a final and binding decision, when necessary. The process usually consists of the neutral helping the parties to frame the issues, sharing information, mediating and settling those points on which agreement can be reached. At the end of the process, the neutral (as an arbitrator) makes decisions on any points on which the parties cannot reach agreement.

Mini-Trial ❖ In a mini-trial, a neutral oversees an abbreviated process similar to a full trial in court, including submission of briefs and exhibits and summary hearings. After that process is complete, the neutral may offer an advisory opinion about the likely outcome of the case. The parties then return to negotiations, with a more realistic understanding of the possible outcomes should negotiations fail. The goal of a mini-trial is to encourage prompt, cost-effective resolution of complex litigation. The mini-trial process can help the parties agree on a fair and equitable settlement of the dispute, and can also help narrow the areas of controversy and dispose of collateral issues, such that any actual trial (if required) may be conducted more efficiently. Because the mini-trial is a relatively elaborate ADR method, it is generally reserved for large disputes.

Multi-Step Dispute Resolution ❖ In a multi-step dispute resolution process, parties agree to engage in a progressive series of dispute resolution procedures. One step typically is some form of negotiation, preferably face-to-face between the parties. If unsuccessful, a second tier of negotiation between higher levels of executives may resolve the matter. The next step may be mediation or another facilitated settlement effort. If no resolution has been reached at any of the earlier stages, the agreement can provide for a binding resolution through arbitration or litigation.

Negotiated Rule-Making ❖ Negotiated rule-making, also known as regulatory negotiation, is an alternative to the traditional means by which government agencies issue regulations after a lengthy notice and comment period. Agency officials and affected parties meet under the guidance of a neutral facilitator to engage in joint negotiation and drafting of an agency rule. The public is then asked to comment further on the proposed rule. By encouraging the participation of interested stakeholders in rule-making, the process can make use of perspectives and expertise beyond the confines of the agency, and can help avoid subsequent litigation over the final rule.

Negotiation ❖ Negotiation takes place whenever parties discuss issues and determine what interests they have in common to arrive at a mutually satisfactory outcome. Negotiation is voluntary, non-adjudicative and informal. Positional negotiations focus on demands and counter-demands of disputing parties, sometimes leading to a bargaining process in which parties trade concessions and demands. Interest-based negotiations focus on the interests underlying each party's position on an issue. The parties explore their needs and concerns, and eventually work on developing mutually acceptable solutions that meet as many of their collective interests as possible.

Neutral ❖ A neutral is an independent third party who acts as a mediator, facilitator, conciliator or arbitrator.

Non-Binding Arbitration ❖ In non-binding arbitration, parties present their facts and positions to a neutral, and the neutral advises the parties as to what he or she feels would be a fair and appropriate resolution of the matter. The parties are free to accept or reject the neutral's advice. The parties generally use the non-binding arbitration decision as a tool in resolving their dispute through negotiation or other means.

Ombudsman ❖ An ombudsman is a third-party neutral who researches complaints and suggests or implements solutions.

The ombudsman is generally appointed by an institution to investigate complaints within the institution and to prevent disputes or facilitate their resolution. The ombudsman may use various ADR mechanisms, such as fact-finding or mediation, in the process of resolving disputes brought to his or her attention. In some countries, ombudsmen are chosen to deal with complaints by the public against administrative injustice, with the power to investigate, criticize and publish reports. A public ombudsman may have some power to recommend the payment of compensation.

Parties ❖ Parties are the disputants in any ADR process.

Partnering ❖ Partnering is typically used as a dispute-prevention method for large construction projects. Before the work starts, parties involved in the project meet. With the help of a neutral, they get to know each other, discuss some of the likely problems in the project, and may even settle on a process to resolve misunderstandings and disputes as the project progresses. The aim is to foster a spirit of mutual cooperation in aid of completion of the project.

Respondent ❖ In arbitration, a respondent is a responding party, also known as a defendant.

Settlement Conference ❖ Settlement conferences are perhaps the most common form of ADR used in federal and state courts in the United States. The classic role of the settlement judge (often a magistrate, who will not try the case) is to articulate non-binding judgments about the merits of the case and to facilitate the trading of settlement offers. Some settlement judges and magistrate judges also use mediation techniques in settlement conferences to improve communication between the parties, probe barriers to settlement, and assist in formulating resolutions. In some courts, a specific judge or magistrate judge is designated as the regular settlement judge. In other courts, the assigned judge (or another judicial officer who will not hear the case) hosts settlement conferences at various points during the litigation, often directly before trial.

Submission ❖ A submission is the filing of a dispute to a dispute resolution process after it arises.

Summary Jury Trial ❖ A summary jury trial (similar to a mini-trial) is a non-binding ADR process used to promote settlement in trial-ready cases headed for protracted jury trials. Part or all of a complex dispute may be submitted to a summary jury trial. After an abbreviated hearing in which counsel present evidence in summary form, the jury renders an advisory verdict. The advisory verdict becomes the basis for subsequent settlement negotiations. If the parties do not reach a settlement, the case proceeds to trial. Because they are costly, summary jury trials are used relatively rarely. Typically, the summary jury trial is reserved for large cases when other settlement efforts have failed and where litigants differ significantly in their predictions about likely jury outcomes.

Terms of Reference ❖ In arbitration proceedings sponsored by the International Chamber of Commerce, the parties and the arbitrators jointly prepare a document, known as the "terms of reference," which includes a summary of each party's claims, and the issues to be decided by the arbitrators.

Two-Track Approach ❖ The two-track approach involves use of ADR processes or traditional settlement negotiations in conjunction with litigation. Often, representatives of the disputing parties who are not involved in the litigation conduct the settlement negotiations or ADR procedure. The negotiation or ADR efforts may proceed concurrently with litigation or during an agreed-upon cessation of litigation.

Bibliography

The following bibliography is a limited selection of the vast quantity of literature and reference materials that are available to assist practitioners and parties in understanding the processes and issues involved in arbitration. This listing is not intended to be definitive, or exhaustive, but rather a potential starting point for further reading and research on arbitration-related issues. As noted at the end of this bibliography, there are a number of other bibliographies that may be useful alternative starting points for such reading and research.

General Texts

Thomas E. Carbonneau, *Cases and Materials on the Law and Practice of Arbitration* (2d ed. 2000).

Stephen K. Huber & E. Wendy Trachte-Huber, *Arbitration: Cases and Materials* (1998).

Rodolphe J.A. de Seife, *Domke on Commercial Arbitration* (1987).

History of Arbitration

William C. Jones, "An Inquiry into the History of the Adjudication of Mercantile Disputes in Great Britain and the United States," 25 U. Chi. L. Rev. 445 (1958).

Bruce H. Mann, "The Formalization of Informal Law: Arbitration Before the American Revolution," 59 N.Y.U. L. Rev. 443 (1984).

Paul Sayre, "Development of Commercial Arbitration Law," 37 Yale L.J. 595 (1928).

Earl S. Wolaver, "The Historical Background of Commercial Arbitration," 83 U. Pa. L. Rev. 132 (1934).

Federal Arbitration Act and Related Statutes

American Arbitration Association, www.adr.org (providing information on alternative dispute resolution statutes in all states).

Federal Arbitration Act, 9 U.S.C. §§ 1-307, text available at www.chamber.se/arbitration.

Alternative Dispute Resolution Act of 1998, 28 U.S.C. §§ 651 et seq.

George Kohlik, *Digest of Commercial Laws of the World: State Variations of Commercial Laws* (1996).

Iamn R. Macneil, Richard E. Speidel & Thomas J. Stipanowich, *Federal Arbitration Law: Agreements, Awards and Remedies Under the Federal Arbitration Act* (1994).

Uniform Arbitration Act, adopted by National Conference of Commissioners on Uniform State Laws (1955), text available at www/webcourt.com/uniformarb, and at the AAA site, www.adr.org.

Rules of Sponsoring Organizations

American Arbitration Association, *Commercial Arbitration Rules,* www.adr.org/rules/commercial.

International Chamber of Commerce, *Rules and Procedures,* www.iccw-bo.org/ court/english/arbitration/rules.

JAMS, *Comprehensive Arbitration Rules and Procedures,* jamsadr.com/comprehensive_arb_rules.

London Court of International Arbitration, *Rules, Recommended Clauses & Costs,* www.lcia-arbitration.com/lcia/rulecost/english.

Fundamental Legal Concepts

Paul H. Haagen, "New Wineskins for New Wine: The Need to Encourage Fairness in Mandatory Arbitration," 40 Ariz. L. Rev. 1039 (1998).

Margaret M. Harding, "The Clash Between Federal and State Arbitration Law and the Appropriateness of Arbitration as a Dispute Resolution Process," 77 Neb. L. Rev. 397 (1998).

Stephen L. Hayford, "Federal Preemption and Vacatur: The Bookend Issues Under the Revised Uniform Arbitration Act," 2001 J. Disp. Resol. 67.

Jean R. Sternlight, *The Basic Structure of the FAA: Possible Challenges to Binding Arbitration Agreements,* 2 Ann. ATLA-CLE 2211 (2000).

Terry L. Trantina, "An Attorney's Guide to Alternative Dispute Resolution (ADR): 'ADR 1.01,'" in *Arbitration of Consumer Financial Services Disputes,* 1102 PLI/Corp. 29 (1999).

Constructing an Arbitration Clause

Neal Blacker, "Drafting the Arbitration/ADR Clause: A Checklist for Practitioners," 46 Prac. Law. 55 (2000).

I. Oliver Dillenz, "Drafting International Commercial Arbitration Clauses," 21 Suffolk Transnat'l L. Rev. 221 (1998).

Alan S. Kaplinsky & Mark J. Levin, "Anatomy of an Arbitration Clause: Drafting and Implementation Issues Which Should Be Considered by a Consumer Lender," SF81 ALI-ABA 215 (2001).

Amy McDowe, "Drafting an Enforceable Mandatory Arbitration Agreement in the Employment Setting," 46 Prac. Law. 39 (2000).

Lucy F. Reed, "Drafting Arbitration Clauses" in *International Business Litigation & Arbitration 2000,* 624 PLI/Lit 563 (2000).

Conducting an Arbitration

Paul D. Carrington, "Virtual Arbitration," 15 Ohio St. J. Disp. Resol. 669 (2000).

Thomas E. Crowley, "The Art of Arbitration Advocacy," 1994 Haw. B.J. 8.

Donald T. DeCarlo, "The Arbitration Process," in *Reinsurance Law & Practice* (PLI 1998).

Jay E. Grenig, *Alternative Dispute Resolution with Forms* (1997).

Confirming and Vacating Arbitration Awards

Olivier Antione, "Judicial Review of Arbitral Awards," 54 Disp. Resol. J. 23 (1999).

Ann C. Hodges, "Judicial Review of Arbitration Awards on Public Policy Grounds: Lessons from the Case Law," 16 Ohio St. J. Disp. Resol. 91 (2000).

Adam Milam, "A House Built on Sand: Vacating Arbitration Awards for Manifest Disregard of the Law," 29 Cumb. L. Rev. 705 (1999).

Leanne Montgomery, "Expanded Judicial Review of Commercial Arbitration Awards—Bargaining for the Best of Both Worlds," 68 U. Cin. L. Rev. 529 (2000).

Erika Van Ausdall, "Confirmation of Arbitral Awards: The Confusion Surrounding Section 9 of the Federal Arbitration Act," 49 Drake L. Rev. 41 (2000).

International Arbitration

Gary B. Born, *International Commercial Arbitration in the United States: Commentary and Materials* (2001).

W. Lawrence Craig, William W. Park & Jan Paulsson, *International Chamber of Commerce Arbitration* (1990).

Andreas F. Lowenfeld, *International Litigation and Arbitration* (1993).

Michael J. Mustill & Stewart C. Boyd, *Commercial Arbitration* (1989).

Alan Redfern & Martin Hunter, *Law and Practice of International Commercial Arbitration* (1991).

W. Michael Reisman, W. Laurence Craig, William Park & Jan Paulsson, *International Commercial Arbitration: Cases, Materials and Notes on the Resolution of International Business Disputes* (1997).

Albert Jan Van Den Berg, *The New York Arbitration Convention of 1958: Towards a Uniform Judicial Interpretation* (1981).

Labor and Employment Arbitration

Richard A. Bales, "Compulsory Arbitration of Employment Claims: A Practical Guide to Designing and Implementing Enforceable Agreements," 47 Baylor L. Rev. 591 (1995).

Richard A. Bales, *Labor and Employment Law Compulsory Arbitration: The Grand Experiment in Employment* (1997).

Tim Bornstein, Ann Gosline & Marc Greenbaum, *Labor and Employment Arbitration* (2d ed. 1997).

Charles J. Coleman & Gerald C. Coleman, "Toward a New Paradigm of Labor Arbitration in The Federal Courts," 13 Hofstra Lab. L.J. 1 (1995).

Frank Elkouri & Edna Elkouri, *How Arbitration Works* (5th ed. 1997).

Joseph Z. Fleming, *Grievances and Arbitration for the Organized Employer,* CA41 ALI/ABA 301 (1995).

Henry S. Kramer, *Alternative Dispute Resolution in the Work Place* (Law Journal Press 1998).

Dennis Nolan, "Labor and Employment Arbitration: What's Justice Got to Do with It?" 53 Disp. Resol. J. 40 (1998).

Ronald Turner, "Employment Discrimination, Labor and Employment Arbitration, and the Case Against Union Waiver of the Individual Worker's Statutory Right to a Judicial Forum," 49 Emory L.J. 135 (2000).

Brian K. Van Engen, "Post-*Gilmer* Developments in Mandatory Arbitration: The Expansion of Mandatory Arbitration of Statutory

Claims and the Congressional Effort to Reverse the Trend," 21 J. Corp. L. 391 (1996).

Consumer Arbitration

American Arbitration Association, *A Due Process Protocol for Mediation and Arbitration of Consumer Disputes,* www.adr.org/education.

Alan S. Kaplinsky & Mark J. Levin, "Consumer Financial Services Arbitration: A Panacea or a Pandora's Box?" 55 Bus. Law. 1427 (2000).

Practising Law Institute, *Arbitration of Consumer Financial Services Disputes* (1999).

Jeremy Senderowicz, "Consumer Arbitration and Freedom of Contract: A Proposal to Facilitate Consumers' Informed Consent to Arbitration Clauses in Form Contracts," 32 Columbia J. L. & Soc. Probs. 275 (1999).

David G. Wirtes, Jr., "Suggestions for Defeating Arbitration," 24 Am. J. Trial Advoc. 111 (2000).

Securities Arbitration

Martin L. Budd, *Securities Industry Arbitration: Recent Developments,* SF51 ALI-ABA 11127 (2001).

National Association of Securities Dealers, *NASD Regulation—Resolving Disputes,* www.nasdr.com.

Practising Law Institute, *Securities Arbitration 2001* (2001).

Securities and Exchange Commission, Office of Investor Education and Assistance, *Guide to Arbitration Procedures,* www.sec.gov/consumer/arbproc.

Ethics and Professional Responsibility

American Arbitration Association, *The Code of Ethics for Arbitrators in Commercial Disputes,* 605 PLI/Lit 385 (1999).

International Chamber of Commerce, *The Arbitral Process and the Independence of Arbitrators* (1991).

Note, "The Standard of Impartiality as Applied to Arbitrators by the Federal Courts and Codes of Ethics," 3 Geo. J. Legal Ethics 821 (1990).

Mark P. Zimmett, *Ethics in International Commercial Litigation and Arbitration,* 648 PLI/Lit 539 (2001).

Arbitration Related Journals

ADR and the Law (American Arbitration Association; Fordham International Law Journal; Fordham Urban Law Journal).

American Review of International Arbitration (Columbia University, Parker School of Foreign and Comparative Law).

Dispute Resolution Journal (American Arbitration Association).

Dispute Resolution Magazine (American Bar Association, Section on Dispute Resolution).

Mealey's International Arbitration Report (Mealey Publications).

Ohio State Journal on Dispute Resolution (Ohio State University).

World Arbitration and Mediation Report (BNA International).

Yearbook: Commercial Arbitration (International Council for Commercial Arbitration).

Recent Supreme Court Decisions

Allied-Bruce Terminix Cos. v. Dobson, 513 U.S. 265, 115 S.Ct. 834, 130 L.Ed.2d 753 (1995) (breadth of commerce power underlying Federal Arbitration Act).

Circuit City Stores, Inc. v. Adams, 532 U.S. 105, 121 S.Ct. 1302, 149 L.Ed.2d 234 (2001) (limits of employment exception to Federal Arbitration Act).

Cortez Byrd Chips, Inc. v. Bill Harbert Construction Co., 529 U.S. 193, 120 S.Ct. 1331, 146 L.Ed.2d 171 (2000) (venue provisions of Federal Arbitration Act).

Doctor's Associates, Inc. v. Casarotto, 517 U.S. 681, 116 S.Ct. 1652, 134 L.Ed.2d 902 (1996) (preemption of state statute inconsistent with Federal Arbitration Act).

Eastern Associated Coal Corp. v. United Mine Workers of America, 531 U.S. 57, 121 S.Ct. 462, 148 L.Ed.2d 354 (2000) (review of labor arbitration award).

EEOC v. Waffle House, Inc., No. 99-1823, 2002 WL 46763 (Jan. 15, 2002) (EEOC ability to pursue employment discrimination claims, despite arbitration agreement).

First Options of Chicago, Inc. v. Kaplan, 514 U.S. 938, 115 S.Ct. 1920, 131 L.Ed.2d 992 (1995) (responsibility for determining arbitrability of disputes).

Gilmer v. Interstate/Johnson Lane Corp., 500 U.S. 20, 111 S.Ct. 1647, 114 L.Ed.2d 26 (1991) (employment arbitration; arbitration of statutory claims).

Green Tree Financial Corp.-Alabama v. Randolph, 531 U.S. 79, 121 S.Ct. 513, 148 L.Ed.2d 373 (2000) (appeals issues; arbitration of statutory claims).

Litton Financial Printing Division v. NLRB, 501 U.S. 190, 111 S.Ct. 2215, 115 L.Ed.2d 177 (1991) (labor arbitration; contractual basis for arbitration).

Major League Baseball Players Ass'n. v. Garvey, 532 U.S. 504, 121 S.Ct. 1724, 149 L.Ed.2d 740 (2001) (review of labor arbitration award).

Mastrobuono v. Shearson Lehman Hutton, Inc., 514 U.S. 52, 115 S.Ct. 1212, 131 L.Ed.2d 76 (1995) (public policy exception to arbitration; arbitrator power to award punitive damages).

Mitsubishi Motors Corp. v. Soler Chrysler-Plymouth, Inc., 473 U.S. 614, 105 S.Ct. 3346, 87 L.Ed.2d 444 (1985) (international arbitration; limits of public policy exception to arbitration).

Rodríguez de Quijas v. Shearson/American Express, Inc., 490 U.S. 477, 109 S.Ct. 1917, 104 L.Ed.2d 526 (1989) (securities arbitration; limits of public policy exception to arbitration).

Shearson/American Express, Inc. v. McMahon, 482 U.S. 220, 107 S.Ct. 2332, 96 L.Ed.2d 185 (1987) (limits of public policy exception to arbitration).

Southland Corp. v. Keating, 465 U.S. 1, 104 S.Ct. 852, 79 L.Ed.2d 1 (1984) (preemption of state law by Federal Arbitration Act).

Vimar Seguros y Reaseguros, S.A. v. M/V Sky Reefer, 515 U.S. 528, 115 S.Ct. 2322, 132 L.Ed.2d 462 (1995) (international arbitration).

Volt Information Sciences, Inc. v. Board of Trustees of Leland Stanford Junior University, 489 U.S. 468, 109 S.Ct. 1248, 103 L.Ed.2d 488 (1989) (application of state law to arbitration, where chosen by parties).

Wright v. Universal Maritime Services Corp., 525 U.S. 70, 119 S.Ct. 391, 142 L.Ed.2d 361 (1998) (public policy exception to arbitration).

Bibliographies

International Commercial Arbitration: Resources in Print and Electronic Format, www.lib.uchicago.edu.

Resources on International Commercial Arbitration (CD-ROM), available from www.kluwerlaw.com.

Hans Smit & Pechota Vratislav, *Commercial Arbitration: An International Bibliography* (1998).

Steven C. Bennett is a native of Minneapolis, Minnesota. Educated at Macalester College (B.A. 1979) and New York University School of Law (J.D. 1984), he clerked for Senior Circuit Judge Carl McGowan (D.C. Circuit Court of Appeals) and was an Assistant United States Attorney in the Southern District of New York.

A partner and general commercial litigator in the New York City offices of Jones, Day, Reavis & Pogue, the author co-teaches the Commercial Arbitration course at Brooklyn Law School. A frequent lecturer at continuing legal education programs, the author has written widely, including numerous articles on arbitration and alternative dispute resolution.